Second Edition

A First-Year
Teacher's
Guidebook

An Educational Recipe Book for Success

Bonnie Williamson

Dynamic Teaching Company
Sacramento, California

A First-Year Teacher's Guidebook, Second Edition

Dynamic Teaching Company, PO Box 276711, Sacramento, CA 95827

Editors: Marilyn Pribus
       Kathy Hoff
Illustrator: Sandy Thornton
Cover design: Robert Howard Graphic Design
Book design & composition: Arrow Graphics, Inc.

Publisher's Cataloging-in-Publication
(*Provided by Quality Books, Inc.*)

Williamson, Bonnie
    A first-year teacher's guidebook: an educational recipe
    book for success/Bonnie Williamson.—2nd ed.
    p. cm.
    Includes bibliographical references and index.
    Preassigned LCCN: 98-70574
    ISBN: 0-937899-39-9

    1. First year teachers—United States—Handbooks,
manuals, etc. 2. Teaching—Handbooks, manuals, etc.
3. Teaching—Aids and devices—Handbooks, manuals, etc.
4. Classroom management. I. Title.

    LB2844.1.N4W55 1998   371.1
                      QBI98-567

Dedication

For my friend and editor, Kathy Hoff

OTHER BOOKS BY BONNIE WILLIAMSON

Classroom Management: A Guidebook for Success
101 Ways to Put Pizazz Into Your Teaching
Parent Power—A Guide to Your Child's Success

Acknowledgements

My sincere thanks to Lynn Pribus, Kathy Hoff, Sandy Thornton Alvart Badalian and Robert Howard. My deep appreciation also goes to teachers and specialists who helped along the way, Jeff Stevens, David and Charlotte Berkham, G. M. Garcia, Keith and Carolyn Johnson, Virginia Cotton, Dr. Dennis Mah, Jan Merle, David Giles, Patty Forester, Char Painter, Pat Holzknecht, Dr. Bonnie Allen, Frank Meder, Sharon Palmer, Stu and Sue Clark, Mary Jo Fennell, Russ Jelsma, Nonie Stevens, Jeanne Lemkuil, Jeff Bartley, Peggy Vest, Dr. Tedford, Barbara Arnold, Karen Kiser, Sharon Zoller, Karen Eckert, Tony Galindo and Laurie Mar. They generously shared their time and knowledge to help make this book possible.

Contents

Preface

Dear Teachers,

My years have been spent teaching in affluent suburbs as well as in inner-city schools with well over half the students from welfare families. Some come from a startling variety of cultures and speak little English.

My own experiences have served me well in writing this book and I've traveled all over the country to interview other teachers to add their points of view to my own.

Teaching has been very important in my life and I feel a little as though I'm passing on a "torch." And as I pass it on, I wish to entrust this book to you—the next group of inspired teachers of young people.

Bonnie Williamson
Sacramento, CA

1

Getting Started

Teaching is rewarding, challenging and fulfilling. You'll also find it can be tough, rough and discouraging. I wrote this book especially to provide vital information to help you in the classroom throughout the year.

This isn't a text. Rather, it's a guidebook—a recipe book, if you will—to give you the necessary ingredients to ensure a successful school year. Use it. Mark in it. Make it yours.

CLASSROOM RECIPE BOOK

 TEACHER TIP: *Some teachers, to make the book easier to use, take it to a print shop and have the spine cut off. Then they ask to have three holes punched so it will fit inside a three-ring binder.*

What Do I Do After I Sign the Contract?

If you're returning to the same school next year, you can skip this part. But if you'll be in a new school and the expense isn't prohibitive, visit it. If you'll be relocating to a new community, be sure to visit your school when you go househunting.

Go for a visit to see:
• Your new town
• The school
• Your room

Before you buy the ticket or fill your car's gas tank, call to see when the school office will be open. (Many school offices don't open until early in August.)

When you call the school, give the secretary your name and tell her how much you're looking forward to being on the faculty. Then tell her the day you'd like to visit and ask for an appointment with the principal. Also tell her you want to pick up all the teacher's editions of books for your particular grade level.

Visiting the School Site

Seeing *your* school for the first time is an exciting experience. As you near the school, look around the neighborhood and get a "feel" for the community. Look at the houses, the children playing in the yards and the types of businesses nearby.

Dress nicely in clothes which would be appropriate in the classroom. Looking good will give you confidence as you meet the principal, secretary and other faculty members who might already be working in their classrooms.

Meeting the Principal

Asking questions not only gets answers but shows you are interested and responsible.

Before you arrive, take time to think over and rehearse what you plan to say. Write out your questions and make a list of things you'll need in your classroom. Then relax.

Naturally, you'll want to leave the principal and others you meet with a good first impression. How? Be enthusiastic, sensitive, friendly and sincere.

TEACHER TIP FOR WOMEN: When meeting a person in authority for the first time, lower the pitch of your voice. Nervous women tend to speak in a high voice, which reduces their ability to communicate from a position of strength. You don't want to speak with a "little girl's" voice.

"Her voice was gentle, soft and low; an excellent thing in a woman."
Shakespeare

When you meet the principal, offer your hand in a firm, but not gripping, handshake and make direct eye contact. Here's a list of questions you should have ready:

- Where's my classroom?
- May I visit it today?
- How many students will I have?

- How much money am I assigned each year per student for supplies?
- Do you have an open-supply room, or must I order supplies?
- How do I arrange for field trips?
- Will I have a classroom aide?
- If so, how many hours a day?
- Will a veteran teacher be assigned to help me this year?
- Are parents supportive of the school program and do any of them help in the classroom?
- Do you have an exchange program for any subjects?
- When will the first faculty meeting be held?
- Do I need to attend an in-service or meetings for new teachers before school begins?
- Is a binder available of all school rules and procedures?
- When will the yard- and bus-duty schedules be posted?
- May I pick up all the teacher's editions of books for my grade today?
- Will I have computers in my classroom?
- Is someone in the district available to help me with computers?
- Is a curriculum guideline available?
- May I check out books from the library now?
- What is the total school enrollment?
- What are the ethnic backgrounds and languages of my students?
- Do I have a bilingual aide?
- What other duties will I have, such as any committees?
- Where do I park?

Who? What? Where? When? How often? Will I? May I? Can I? You bet!

TEACHER TIP: You'll find that school equipment frequently doesn't work. One way to save yourself hours of frustration in the years ahead from trying to coax broken, worn-out equipment to work is to itemize your equipment needs. Then, beginning with your first year, buy one of the items for yourself. This might be a cassette recorder and extension cord. Be sure to engrave your driver's license number on it with an electric pen, in case it's stolen.

Invest in your *own* equipment, year-by-year. I've saved so much time by having my personal pencil sharpener, paper cutter and cassette player.

The School Secretary

One of the most important people on your staff is the school secretary. Make friends with this VIP on your first visit and be friendly, warm and receptive to advice. She can answer numerous questions for you.

- Where's my mailbox?
- When do I get my classroom key?
- Must I sign in each day? If so, where?
- Must I sign up for lunch? Where?
- May I have a schedule for the first day? The first week?
- May I have a copy of the lunch schedule for the month?
- When will I receive my class list? My register?
- Where will the duty schedule be posted?
- How much do students pay for lunch? For milk? For reduced lunch?
- Who collects the lunch or milk money?
- Where do parents get free-lunch forms?
- When is the school nurse here?
- Where are the permanent-record folders kept for my class?
- May I have a list of the faculty and staff?
- Where is the work area for teachers? Do we have a copier?
- How do I order films and VCR tapes?
- Where do I find the overlays for my overhead projector? Do you have a Thermofax™ to make masters?
- Do you have resource teachers or special programs here at the school?

You can get local maps on the World Wide Web. Larger city newspapers are often on-line, too.

Before you leave, give your address and telephone number to the secretary. Ask her to contact you with any other information you should know before you return.

Getting Acquainted with the Community

If you'll be in a new community, consider subscribing to its newspaper during the summer before you begin teaching. This is an outstanding way to learn about school-board meetings, listings of houses and apartments to rent and local goings-on. You can also visit the postcard section of a nearby drug store and pick up several cards highlighting community interests.

♣ HINT: If you're unable to make the trip early, write the Chamber of Commerce in your new town for maps and resources.

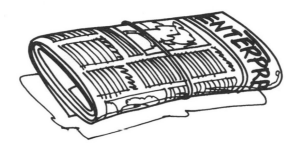

Begin Planning for the First Semester

After your first visit to the school, organize your thoughts and materials and order necessary supplies.

- Outline what you'll be doing the first month in reading, math and language. Order any supplies or audiovisual materials you'll need. Check to see if appropriate computer software programs are available.

- After reading the teacher's edition of your science book, plan a short science unit for September, including the bulletin boards you'll use, films to order and VCR tapes and filmstrips to go along with the unit.

- Decide on activities related to that unit. If you plan a unit on fish, for instance, see if you can arrange a field trip to an aquarium or a fish hatchery.

- Coordinate art, math, reading and spelling activities with your science unit.

Well-laid plans will smooth the start of school.

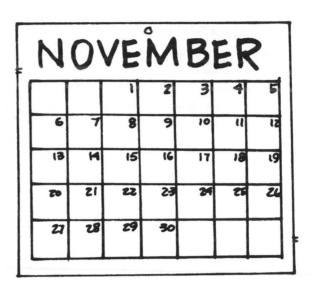

♣ HINT: Consider selecting a monthly theme in either science or social studies. You can change your own routine each month and your students will enjoy the subjects more. Go to your nearest teacher bookstore for ideas and materials.

Your success as a new teacher will depend upon how well you perform your job during the first year. You need to know what your school expects, what you expect and what you can reasonably accomplish. Remember that you can never be perfect, but strive to do a good job. It will take lots of planning and hard work, but *you* can do it!

Organizing Your Classroom

Setting up your classroom can be an exciting adventure. As with your home, your room at school reflects you—your personality, your creativity and your needs.

In this chapter you'll find a number of different ways to organize a classroom. All have been used successfully. Use this chapter as a road map along your personal pathway to a well-functioning classroom.

NOTE: Due to the rapid increase in enrollments in some schools you may find your class in the cafeteria, the school library or gym. If this happens, arrange the desks the best you can. Be sure all students can see you at all times and that you will be able to move from desk-to-desk quickly. This will help with your classroom management.

Desk Arrangements

First decide how you will be using the classroom. Do you plan to use desks? How? Will you need a table for your reading circle? For your aide?

Since September will involve teaching rules and procedures and you will need the constant attention of the entire class, you may

Your classroom blueprint (plan/ arrangement) is likely to change during the year. Some teachers even use several arrangements in the same day.

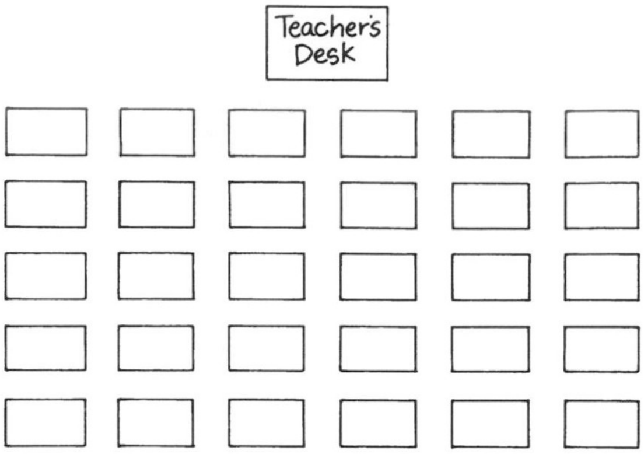

Teacher's Desk

Drawing A: The traditional classroom's focus is to the front of the room. Some teachers prefer this arrangement for the opening weeks of school while teaching rules and procedures.

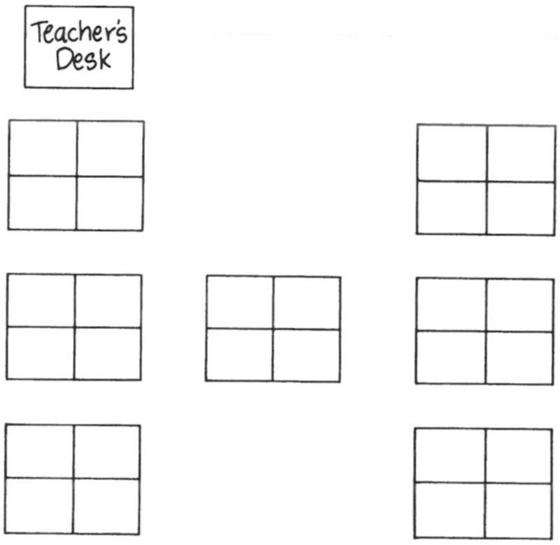

Teacher's Desk

Drawing B: This room is arranged for students to work in small groups.

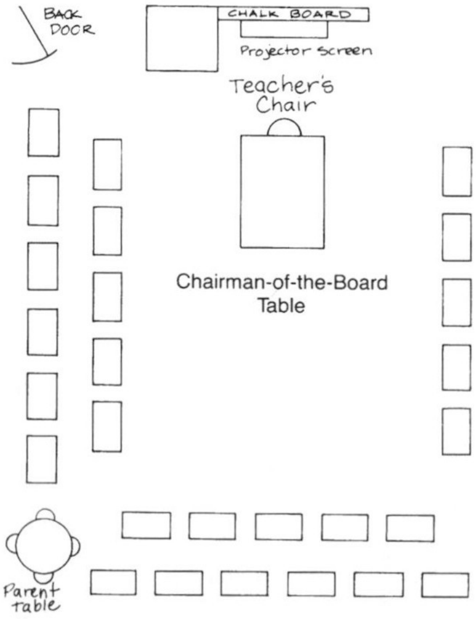

BACK DOOR

CHALK BOARD

Projector Screen

Teacher's Chair

Chairman-of-the-Board Table

Parent Table

Drawing C: Desks are arranged in three groups, or stations. All desks in back rows are arranged so students have a clear view of the teacher and chalkboard.

choose to begin with the traditional rows in your classroom. Later, you may change to stations, or other arrangements.

Some teachers strongly prefer one particular plan, while others may use several different ones during the year.

No matter which arrangement you use, place the students' desks so you can oversee the room at all times. The students must be able to see you, too, whether you are at the chalkboard, the overhead or using a wall map. Always leave enough space between desks to get to individual students.

Group-learning classroom In this classroom students may work in pairs or small groups. This model enables students to work freely together, to exchange ideas and support each other. For an in-depth look on how to arrange your classroom into learning groups, see the chapter on Classroom Management.

If you have a split class, students from different grades, this model works particularly well, as the stations can handily group students by grade level.

A table at the back is useful for:
• A small reading group
• Parent helpers, cross-age tutors or an aide

Arranging Equipment

Some teachers use only the chalkboard or marlite board each day while others prefer the overhead projector, or both. If possible, store your overhead on a cart out of classroom traffic patterns. The same is true for computers, TVs and VCRs.

Keep your cassette tape recorder or CD player where it will be used. This is often determined by the location of electrical outlets.

Another vital piece of equipment is the pencil sharpener. The standard crank-type sharpener often works poorly and can contribute to behavior problems. Consider purchasing your own electric pencil sharpener for the classroom.

For P.E. equipment, place a large cardboard box or mesh bag in the back of the room.

Student storage spaces Be sure you have a place where students can keep their jackets, backpacks, umbrellas and boots. See that the hooks are the right height so students can easily hang personal items.

Activity table If you have room for an extra table, you'll find it useful for projects such as crossword puzzles, temporary science displays or a center with cassette tapes and headsets for small groups.

♣ HINT: Consider placing 3-D puzzles at a learning center. The larger ones can take hours to construct while the small puzzles require less than 30 minutes. Game stores carry these puzzles. Three popular designs are of the White House, Empire State Building and a Mississippi River steamboat. After completion, students can spray the upright puzzle (often with 800 pieces), with a laminating spray. This can also be purchased at game stores.

Another great game for students to play at an activity center comes from Gamewright and is called rat-a-tat CAT™.

Storing Classroom Supplies

In order for your classroom to function efficiently, you'll need to have many supplies on hand. Some items are used over again from year-to-year while others, such as pencils, seem to evaporate in seconds. Tracking these supplies is like running a large warehouse single-handedly.

Paper supplies For paper set aside at least one large drawer within easy reach of your students and provide a selection of the following:

- Penmanship writing paper
- Notebook paper
- Math, language and spelling paper
- Art paper

Your "student-paper drawer" should be kept well-stocked and open for all students to use. You may designate a student to keep it neat and filled.

You're not only the teacher, you're the quartermaster and director of supplies.

♣ HINT: One teacher purchases an eight-compartment shoe-storage box to store papers used in the classroom. This unit is placed on a table near her desk.

You'll need a large drawer for your own use, too. Use it to store sentence strips, tagboard and bulletin board supplies.

☜ NOTE: Ask a student in your local high school to construct a wooden cabinet for student mailboxes. Place each student's name on an individual box and use for all materials that need to go home.

TEACHER TIP: The most convenient place to store all charts is in a closet in your classroom. Purchase pant hangers and hang your charts on them. This keeps them safe and clean. Develop an "index" system by color coding or using index cards. If you don't have a closet, stand charts between file cabinets.

Charts you'll need:
- Reading, phonics, spelling and math
- Science, health and social studies

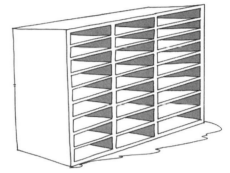

Small-item supplies Start collecting small boxes and coffee cans. Covered with bright plastic adhesive paper, they can be useful for the many small items in your classroom, including beans used to teach math.

Clear plastic jars make excellent storage containers. Most small items can also be kept in small drawers. If having them at grabbing level creates problems, place them in boxes or cans on a higher shelf or cupboard. Always have extra supplies available for new students who enter your classroom.

Cleaning supplies The logical place to store your cleaning supplies is under the sink if you have one. Besides cleanser, soap and sponges, you may want an old, working iron for art projects.

Computer supplies Computer supplies require a little more specialized care than other materials.

Computer screens need to be cleaned often by using an anti-static cloth or sponge. The sponge is useful as it can be washed and reused. Other products which are useful for screens are all-purpose cleaning wipes (use static-free only) or look for an anti-static cleaning and dusting spray. These can be purchased at computer stores.

Itty-bitty odds and ends: Pencils, erasers, scissors, rulers, crayons, paints, glue, staples, pins, thumbtacks, paper clips, big clips, adhesive bandages, safety pins, transparent tape and small nails

♣ HINT: Some manufacturers provide a selection of computer cleaning supplies in large plastic tubs. Look for these at computer stores.

Keyboards can be kept free from dust by using a mini vacuum on the keyboard. This can also be purchased at a computer store.

Keeping disks free from dust and dampness is vital in the classroom. Look for multimedia storage boxes which hold up to 160 disks such as CDs, diskettes and Zip™ disks.

If at all possible, keep computer supplies near the computers. This will facilitate the upkeep and care of your computers and their supplies by your students.

You'll find that having everything carefully organized will make your job much easier when you already have numerous other things to think about. You don't want to wonder where you put a particular teaching aid or necessary student supplies when you are hurriedly getting ready for a lesson.

Headsets must be kept clean at all times with a disinfectant to prevent the spread of head lice among students.

3

Preparations for Opening Day

Whether you're a brand new teacher or a veteran, the week before school starts can be overwhelming. In this chapter, however, we'll cut your massive job of final preparation into manageable bits and pieces.

By this time you'll probably have your furniture ready for the opening of school. You've found a place for your equipment, a table for parents and small groups and, perhaps a listening or math center. You've also left open spaces near high traffic areas such as drinking fountains and wastebaskets.

Now comes the final countdown for putting up bulletin boards, arranging your files and desk and organizing your classroom library. First impressions are important and since you want your classroom to be inviting and stimulating, you should decorate with warmth, color and pizazz.

TEACHER TIP: All teachers should enlist the help of an eager teen for the week before school begins. If you don't have your own, rent one! A promise of money and lunch at a fast-food place makes many neighborhood young people eager to be your temporary assistant to put out books, organize materials and be an all-around "go-fer."

Bulletin Boards

During your teaching career, you'll spend hours putting up and taking down bulletin boards. At the beginning of school, however, leave several boards blank. On the first day, toss out a couple ideas and let your students create boards for you.

Tips for bulletin boards

- Use to introduce a new unit.
- Boards need to be attractive and serve as a teaching tool.
- Commercial bulletin boards can be purchased at teacher stores.
- You can design and create your own.
- Students can create boards for you.
- A parent volunteer, under your direction, can assemble your boards.
- Always set aside one board where students pick out their own good work to post.

TEACHER TIP: Keep an ongoing notebook filled with your outstanding bulletin board ideas. Jot down measurements and draw a simple design of your favorites. Also take a picture of the finished board for your notebook.

Time-saver ideas for fantastic bulletin boards

- Select a title. Have your helper put the letters for it in order, then paper clip each word together to form the caption.
- Jot down the dimensions of your board before going to measure and cut the paper.
- Pull a desk next to the bulletin board for your supplies as you work.
- If you have several bulletin boards, consider assigning a theme for each or use one theme each month.
- Buy an apron with large pockets to keep scissors, stapler and pencil handy as you work.
- When using pins, wear a pincushion on your wrist. Cover your pin-pushing finger with a thimble or piece of masking tape. Some teachers like staples or thumbtacks better than pins.
- Use colorful fabric.
- Wallpaper makes a great background.
- Display work from a clothesline.
- Laminate the bulletin board pieces to preserve them.

Teacher's bulletin board You'll need a bulletin board near your desk for lunch and speech schedules, a *copy* of your teaching credential to show you are a professional and other notes to yourself.

➤ NOTE: Be sure to place a small bulletin board near the door for lunch menus and activity calendars each month for student and parent reference. Allow space for a "Student-of-the-Week" picture and story.

You may use the space above chalkboards for the alphabet and numbers. Some teachers prefer the colorful ones from teacher bookstores.

♣ HINT: Don't forget to put up the flag in the wall holder.

Invest in a hand-held staple gun. This works far better than the stapler supplied by most school districts.

TEACHER TIP: Make friends with your nearest teacher-bookstore staff. Each year you may need to replenish your bulletin board materials and supplies. If you're not near a store, ask other teachers what they do or log onto the Internet for a catalog or suggestions from teachers elsewhere.

Special Storage

File cabinet Organize your file cabinet before school begins. It's handy to color code your materials by subject. Put math items in red folders, reading in blue and language in yellow, for example.

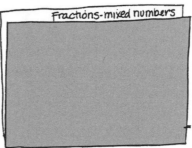

Student work You need a system for students to use each day for turning in specific items and receiving graded papers. The latter can be placed in student mailboxes or a student can return them.

Incoming papers/money

- Students could place homework under a paperweight each morning at a designated place.
- Money for book orders should go into a specific box.
- Notes from parents should go into a separate box near the teacher's desk.

Closet items You'll need a mirror hanging inside the door, a broom, dustpan, extra hangers, apron and an old pair of shoes. Plastic disposable gloves should be used for bloody noses and "throw-ups."

Classroom Supplies

While you'll want materials convenient for students, you'll also want to be able to monitor them.

Supply table

- Select a table with easy access.
- Set the table apart with a colorful place mat.
- Keep pencils in a mug.
- Fill a basket with extra crayons.
- Have a basket available for broken pencils, extra scissors, crayons and erasers.
- Fill a small basket with slips of paper for writing notes, spelling out words and ballots for voting.
- Clearly label your own pencils and scissors.

♣ HINT: If possible, have students buy their own schoolboxes to hold pencils, scissors and erasers. When children don't have the money for this box, the PTA and some churches will often supply them.

Have the class decide how to discourage students from hoarding supplies.

☛ NOTE: Post a sign on all drawers and cupboards to list supplies inside. This is helpful for student monitors who pass out paper and art materials.

Place pencils with points up. Otherwise, students will turn over each pencil, looking for the sharpest point.

Charts and maps
All charts needed for the first day should be in place prior to the opening of school. Decide if you'll use the charts on chart stands or on hooks above the chalkboard. Some of your charts might be:

- A weather map
- A flannelboard
- Charts illustrating colors, counting, shapes, vowels and consonants, as needed
- Grade two upward—a multiplication chart (cover when testing)
- A globe and state and world maps, as needed

Library
Provide your students with a reading center where they can sit and enjoy books from the classroom library.

Students should be able to reach the books easily and linger long enough to make their selections. Keep the library out of heavy traffic patterns. Set up a simple system to sign out books to take home as well. You may lose some books, but you'll enable your students to discover the joy of reading.

A library is a cafeteria for the mind.

L. Pribus

Your desk
Stock your desk with a treasure chest of necessary supplies like paper clips, thumbtacks, note pads, pencils (black,

Get your books from garage sales, teachers who retire, parent- and student- donations and book club memberships.

red and blue), pens (colored for grading), overhead-projector pens, permanent markers, stapler, staples, staple remover, large scissors, ruler, paper punch, masking tape, transparent tape, colored paper clips for page markers and a timer.

You'll either need to get a lesson-plan book or design your own. Some teachers now do plans on their computers. You'll need a record book for grades, class-attendance register, a folder for substitute information, teacher's book for each subject, current read-aloud book, dictionary and thesaurus.

Get Ready, Get Set...Go

Before the opening of school, write your name, grade level and room number, along with the first week's schedules on the chalkboard. This will answer many questions for parents and students on the first day. Also, put up a "Welcome" sign at the front of the classroom.

Decide how much help you'll need the first week to pass out papers, run errands and take out P.E. equipment. If possible, have the previous teacher look over your class list and indicate dependable students to do these chores. Then write the jobs on the chalkboard and students' names after each one. You must have help each day, particularly the first week.

Other jobs must also be done before school starts.

- Write lesson plans for the first day and first week. Plan more lessons than you think you'll need.

- Be sure you prepare many short activities such as crossword puzzles, bingo games and song sheets. Pick out a couple songs and find recordings to go with them. Make copies of the lyrics for students to use until they learn the words.

- If you plan to use a film, video or CD the first week, sign up now. At some schools you must sign up a week or more ahead to get the hour and day you wish.

TEACHER TIP: *To simplify your future teaching, keep a copy of the film and video invoices you use the first year. The next year you can simply pull out the invoices and fill out a new form.*

- Choose a spot in the room where you'll stand so your students will always know they must be quiet and wait for an important announcement. You may wish to place a small masking tape "X" on the spot.

- To get your students' attention, decide on alternate methods such as sounding a bell, striking a note on the piano, switching the light off and on or raising your hand.

- Be prepared to deal with visitors or other interruptions. Should students continue to work?

- Determine how and when you'll take lunch count and attendance. Will students sign in? Will they sign up for lunch or will you ask them to raise their hands? Will you ask a monitor to be in charge of the lunch and milk routine? Write down what the younger ones order for lunch, as they often forget.

- Decide what to do about absent students. Will you assign a buddy to take homework to them or will the parents come for it? How long will you give to make up missed work?

- Plan for transitions in the classroom when you change from one subject to the next. How will you do this and still maintain order? One teacher, for example, has her fourth graders put away their language books and take out math books, paper and pencil before the recess bell rings so they are ready to begin math when they return from recess.

TEACHER TIP: *Choose your method of having students respond to questions. Will they raise their hands? Do a "thumbs up" and "down" for yes and no answers? Will they use sign-language symbols for the deaf for "yes" and "no"? Research indicates that teachers call on students who they feel know the answer. Also, studies say we tend to call on boys most often. This needs to change.*

Yes   *No*

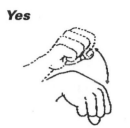 

Remind yourself:
"I am a confident,
effective teacher."
"I am positive,
patient and
enthusiastic."

- Decide how your students will move in and out of small groups. Have a firm plan to cut down on noise, poking and running.

- Devise your end-of-day routine. Will your students sing a "goodbye" song? Will you do a short summary of what they learned that day? How about using a theme from the day to play Trivial Pursuit™? Have a plan for cleaning your room. Who will do this? What about having a helper board? If you don't insist upon a routine, you'll be stuck. Your students can learn a great deal about responsibility through the procedures you establish in the classroom.

- Prepare a short "Welcome" letter to hand out to students and parents the first day.

- Choose the management system you'll be using. See the chapter on Classroom Management for suggestions.

- Have a chart in the room to illustrate voice levels.

- Decide if you want to look at your students' permanent records before school begins. Some teachers prefer to wait a few weeks, but you need to know about any students with physical problems.

- Prepare nameplates for each desk.

- Be sure you have two copies of the class list.

- Have some method for taking attendance the first day.

- Pick up your grade book from the office and place it inside your desk.

Personal preparation Before school opens you'll need to prepare yourself mentally and emotionally for your new experience.

- Visualize yourself as being competent and serene in your classroom.
- Read some "happy messages" from former students or friends.
- Write positive statements such as, "I empower my students to be great learners. I am confident and happy today."
- Provide your new staff with a tray of your favorite cookies or fruit.
- Take an "after-recess treat" for your students. They'll be very hungry the first day.

Say, "I have high standards for my students and I help them reach their goals."

TEACHER TIP: *Ask your school office if a veteran teacher is available to help you during the year. Also, some districts assign mentor teachers to come to your school and help new teachers.*

Personal-reward system Use a bingo board to help with your many duties as you open the year. An illustrated sample board is partially prepared.

B	I	N	G	O
Order films		Put up one bull bd.		Have coffee with my mentor
Bake cookies for faculty		FREE	Make extra copy class list	
		Write mon. memo		Buy crackers
Buy stapler	Order overhead pens		Run songs	

As soon as you do one job, "X" it out. After doing five in a row give yourself a treat. This might be buying a new book, having your hair done, buying a new putter for your golf game or spending a stress-free weekend at your favorite hideaway.

Another stress reducer is to have a stamp made of your name. During your years as a teacher, you'll write your name thousands of times on report cards, deficiency notices and other messages. Have a name stamp made and splurge on one that is self-inking. This will help keep your name legible and save you from writer's cramp!

Your success during the new school year will depend upon how well you prepare ahead. Know what your expectations are and make sure you have everything you'll need to help meet them. Realize it's up to you to guide your students through another year on their educational journey. Enlist their help and cooperation to keep the trip as storm-free as possible.

First Day

Today is Jennifer's first day as a certificated teacher after student teaching for three quarters. Except for a few butterflies, she feels ready to face her second graders. She graduated from the university in June and was hired in July so she has had eight weeks to prepare. She believes her first day will be successful.

Angelo has been a substitute teacher in a large metropolitan school district since graduating from college last December, but he wants to teach full time. Yesterday, the school district asked him to substitute in a fourth-grade classroom until a permanent teacher could be hired and told him he might apply for the position. Angelo feels nervous and unprepared. With only seven hours' notice he barely had time to get supplies, tack up a bulletin board and scribble a few lesson plans.

Laura, 35, is entering teaching for the first time. Two years ago she returned to college to complete her major in education and chose her final student teaching at the kindergarten level, her first love. However, this morning she'll be facing pre-adolescent sixth graders. Becoming a teacher in a new city (where her husband transferred to an excellent job) means that Laura will be team teaching 70 students a day. She, like Angelo, is apprehensive and yet hopeful.

It's normal to be anxious. It's OK to make mistakes.

Beginner's Job Feelings

No matter if it's your first day as a student teacher, a substitute or a new teacher, you'll likely experience feelings of inadequacy, anxiety and some fear. This is perfectly normal. Remind yourself frequently that, "It's all right to be a beginner; it's OK to make mistakes."

Every teacher has had a first day of teaching.

One way to feel good is for women to buy a new dress and for men to buy a new sports jacket and slacks. Since most students wear new clothes to school the first day, why don't you? It will give you a lift, make you feel businesslike and can help to make your first day even more successful.

🍎 *TEACHER TIP: Keep a pair of thoroughly comfortable shoes at school. You'll be walking many miles and some days your feet will let you know it! It's a relief to slide into some old familiar footwear.*

A Recipe for Success

In this chapter you'll learn how to move through this most important day with confidence, courage and self-assurance. Underline important passages; use the lists in this chapter as checksheets; add to my notes in the margins. Doing this, in itself, will help you feel much more in control and prepared to meet that first class.

First-Day Checklist

- Do I have duty of any kind today? When?
- Do I have enough books for each student and extras for newcomers?
- Do I have copies of my class list?
- Do I have a name tag ready for each student?

- Do I need to pick up either a TV or VCR for any lesson I'm teaching today?
- Are all desk supplies ready? Do I have enough pencils, erasers, rulers, scissors and crayons for each student?
- Do I have art paper ready for art projects?
- Do I have a sheet ready for taking attendance?
- Do I have a timer to alert my class for recess and lunch?
- Do I have change for milk/lunch money?
- Did I bring a nutritious snack for myself?

Arrange to be at school *at least* one hour before the students arrive. This will give you time to go over lesson plans, check your mailbox for important messages, be sure all materials are in order to be passed out in the room and catch your breath.

If you have yard or bus duty the first morning, you'll need to allow even more extra time.

> Always be on time for yard duty. When you're late, you delay other teachers. Be considerate and be prompt. This is part of your professional duty.

Meet Parents

Many parents, particularly in the primary grades, bring their children to school the first day. Some will be waiting at your classroom door, while others will arrive late and knock.

Many schools prepare an information sheet for each child to take home at the end of the first day. However, parents who come early with their children want to know NOW what is going to happen this first day of school. There are typical questions they'll ask you. Be prepared!

- When is lunch today?
- What will be served in the cafeteria today?
- Do you have a menu you could give me now?
- When will school be out today? Tomorrow? Usually?
- What supplies should my son bring to school tomorrow?
- When can I talk with you about a problem my daughter had at her last school?
- When can I schedule a conference with you?
- When is Back-to-School Night?
- Do you need a volunteer to help in the classroom today? This year?
- What reading group will my child be in?
- Will my child work on a computer this year?
- Where can I get a form for free lunch for my child?

> Ask a teacher who had your students last year to suggest a parent who might help in your classroom. The parent can:
> • Answer the door.
> • Answer questions.
> • Run interference for you.

It's sad but sometimes true, that faculty rooms are filled with staff members speaking in negative tones—smile and stay positive.

If you read Chapters One and Three carefully, you'll know how to answer these questions or where to find the answers.

Allow ten extra minutes *every* morning to relax in the faculty room before you begin your teaching day. This will give you the opportunity to chat with your fellow faculty members and catch your breath before you meet your students. Pamper yourself.

As the first bell rings, walk confidently to where your students are to line up. If they're waiting outside the classroom, *smile* and introduce yourself to the students and parents standing there.

Before you go inside, tell the students exactly what to do after they walk in the door. This will provide a sense of stability and set an orderly pace for the day.

One teacher who prefers to use assigned seats has her students stand in the back while she points out the cupboard for lunches and hooks on the wall for hanging coats and backpacks. After three children put up their things, she leads them to their assigned seats. This continues until all seats are filled.

Ten extra minutes in your plans give you time to:
• Change a soiled tie.
• Replace panty hose with a run.
• Start your day on time and *relaxed.*

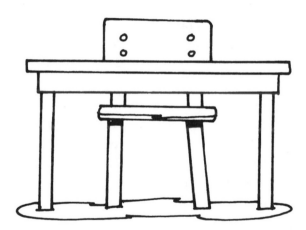

Another teacher points out a shelf for lunches and hooks for coats and says, "Put your lunches away, then choose a seat which fits you and you may sit there." You must decide what system you'll use in your room.

After your class is seated, be sure each student's chair and desk are the proper height. Make necessary adjustments if you can; otherwise notify the custodian.

It's helpful both for you and substitutes to have nameplates on each desk. These can be purchased at teacher stores or made out of sentence strips or tagboard and laminated for long-term use. In primary grades write in manuscript with a felt pen, and in cursive for intermediate.

Establish a Pattern to Start Every Day

Students work well when they know the schedule for each day. This is particularly true the first day and serves as a "comfort zone" for them. Not all teachers continue writing it, but many feel it's worthwhile.

A regular routine in the primary grades lends daily structure and stability. In many children's worlds today, their only source of a stable environment is the classroom. Do everything you can to help them feel comfortable and secure with you. Here's a typical primary morning routine:

- Welcome the class.
- Have students greet you.
- Salute the flag.
- Sing a song.
- Take roll.
- Talk about the calendar and weather.
- Take the lunch and milk counts.
- Collect homework.
- Review the daily schedule.

Some suggestions for the intermediate grades include:

- Salute the flag.
- Begin each morning with two "sponges." A sponge is a tiny bit or piece of information squeezed into a small time segment. Example: Name all the states beginning with the letter, "A."
- Review the daily schedule.
- Begin the lesson at once.
- Take roll later in the morning.
- Begin the day with a brief talk about a Current Event presented by the teacher.

How many states' names start with the letter, "M"?

Get Acquainted with the Classroom

Students will feel much more comfortable when they know where things are kept and they learn the classroom rules. Certain items and locations should be pointed out the first day:

- Teacher's desk: Talk about your rules regarding students getting things out of your desk.

- Where paper, extra pencils, erasers and crayons are kept
- Where physical education equipment is stored
- Where class library books are kept
- Where to find supplies for cleaning up spills, the sink and dirty desks
- The drinking fountain: Let the class know your rules.
- Restroom passes: Discuss rules for going to the bathroom. Do students go alone or with others? Talk about playing in the bathroom.

Emphasize the importance of using the bathroom at recess and lunch break, not on class time.

Hall Passes

Office
Computer
Girls
Boys

- Pencil sharpener: Discuss your rules.
- Paper towel dispenser
- Cassette player, CDs, TV and video: Go over your rules for use.

Get Acquainted with the School

Before the first recess break, it's important that all students, particularly new ones, know where the restrooms are. In many schools, certain restrooms are for primary students only, while others are designated for intermediate students. Your students need to know the proper restroom to use.

It's also necessary for students to know where to line up when the fire bell rings. Take your class on a walking tour and point out the spot where they should go. Then take a few minutes to explain the fire-drill rules for walking out, standing and what signal to listen for to return to the classroom.

There are additional places students need to know about the first day:

- The school office and the principal's office
- Playground and outside drinking fountains
- Various sections such as the preschool, kindergarten, primary and intermediate classrooms
- A designated spot on the playground where you'll pick up your class after recess and lunch
- The area where bus students must wait for the bus
- Cafeteria

Pick the "designated spot" and spray paint it through a soup can with both ends cut out. Check first with your school's office.

Important People at the School

Each school has a support staff and your students need to meet them.

- The principal
- The school secretary, who can explain office rules such as student use of the telephone
- The school nurse
- The custodian
- The bus driver

Use the time walking around the school to stress the rules for each area such as the bus stop and the cafeteria.

♣ HINT: Students come to you with "summer-time stomachs." Remind them on the first days of school that "We're now going out for recess. This is *not* lunch." I've had students dash home thinking it must be lunch time.

Introductions Are in Order

Primary An early priority is to get acquainted with your students. Ask them to introduce themselves while you write their names on the chalkboard or overhead for all to see. At the same time, you can be taking notes on a card indicating any problems such as a child needing help with speech.

Intermediate Ask your students to introduce themselves to the student sitting on their right. Tell them to ask that student to tell them something interesting about himself or herself during recess. When they come back, each student should introduce his or her new acquaintance to the class. You may wish to take notes during the introductions if you see or hear any specific problems.

K.I.S.S. – Keep It Short and Simple

For the first hour you've done most of the talking. Now it's time for the students to start working.

You must keep two things in mind:

- Your students have been on summer vacation. They're used to playing around and not doing much work.
- They're used to being home where they have freedom to eat and go to the bathroom as they please.

To help your students function efficiently, introduce "school" to them in short and simple doses.

Remind your students to get eight-to-ten hours' sleep each night in order to *be sharp* and *stay sharp* at school.

TEACHER TIP: *In the primary grades prepare a memo, or help your students write a note home, asking parents to let them bring one item for a snack each day for the first week of school. Recommend fruit rather than sweets. This snack after recess will carry them through until lunch.*

In the intermediate grades, plan to show an interesting film or video the first day. Purchase a large bag of popcorn and serve in small bowls or small bags.

NOTE:: It's important that your students go home the first day with some schoolwork in their hands. This might be a simple paragraph from a language lesson, a math page or a new book.

Art Lesson

A short art lesson is ideal for introducing students to the new school year.

Primary Set aside a "Good-Work" board and ask students to draw a picture of something they did during the summer to post on the board.

Use bright, colored yarn to mark off squares on your Good-Work board.

Intermediate Ask students to make posters illustrating playground rules. Place some of the posters in the classroom and ask at the office if some might hang in the cafeteria and hallways.

Teacher

While students are busy doing art work, check your class list. Usually a runner will come by to pick up the list for office and district use.

Enjoy your first day; normally it's quiet. Students are in a new room, often with new students and teacher. Also, most are eager to please. Use this eagerness to help get your rules and procedures in place.

The first morning may seem eight hours long, not only to the students but to you. Don't be surprised if your feet hurt and your voice grows weary. Be sure to bring yourself a nutritious, energy-boosting treat to enjoy on your first recess break.

Keep a box of graham crackers in your desk. They'll be a pickup for you, as well as a hungry child.

TEACHER TIP: *Keep a timer on your desk. As soon as you come back from morning recess, set the timer to ring 5-7 minutes before lunch so that if you're busy, it will alert you to stop. You'll have time to get desks cleared, lunches ready to go and students lined up. The timer is a wonderful reminder when students must leave the room to see the resource specialist or you need to time tests or be ready to watch a particular lesson on television.*

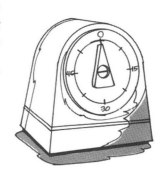

What-Do-I-Do-Now-Teacher Syndrome

Next to, "Hey, teacher, I gotta' go to the bathroom," (frequently said two minutes after coming in from recess) a teacher dreads hearing, "I'm finished. What can I do now?" Veteran teachers use several ideas.

- A child excelling in reading or math can serve as a tutor to other students.
- The student can visit the learning centers you've placed around the room.
- Have a box filled with enrichment pages such as crossword puzzles, color-in math sheets or science work sheets.

One of my students was a "whiz-kid" at math. She loved being a tutor.

Lunch Break

The first-day lunch schedule will vary from school-to-school and district-to-district. Many districts often have a lunch period the first day even if the school is on a shortened schedule and the students go home after lunch.

Set your timer to go off 5-7 minutes before the lunch period begins. Remind those going home directly after lunch to take home all books needed for homework that night. They also must take their lunches, coats and backpacks with them, as they'll leave school from the cafeteria.

If your students will return to the classroom after lunch, assign one child to take out P.E. equipment to use during the lunch period. Also, remind students buying lunch to take their money, and those with lunches to take them. It's very disturbing to lock the room and get almost to the cafeteria before a student says, "Oh, I left my lunch (or money) in the classroom."

When it's time to leave for lunch, line up students in small orderly groups. This might be by rows, stations or tables. Assign a student familiar with the school to lead the class *slowly* to the cafeteria while you walk at the end of the line to oversee lagging, disruptive students.

Many teachers find that the ideal time to read aloud to their students is after lunch. Many say that one of their greatest joys in teaching is this daily sharing of a good book. Don't miss this wonderful opportunity to enrich your students' lives by making a story come alive each day.

Outstanding Read-Aloud Books

The following are teacher-tested read-alouds I've enjoyed reading to my students and other books suggested by veteran teachers and librarians.

♣ HINT: Some publishers are now putting the first chapter of new books on the Internet. This is an outstanding way to preview books. Also, look for reviews posted on the publishers' home pages.

> As a teacher, you'll need to quickly develop patience.

Kindergarten

The Napping House by Audrey Wood

The Wolf's Chicken Stew by Keiko Kasza

Brown Bear, Brown Bear, What Do You See?
    by Bill Martin, Jr.

Corduroy by Don Freeman

Danny and the Dinosaur by Syd Hoff

The Vanishing Pumpkin by Tony Johnston

*Alexander and the Terrible, Horrible, No Good, Very
    Bad Day* by Judith Viorst

Flossie and the Fox by Patricia McKissack

Race of Toad and Deer by Pat Mara

Curious George by H. A. Rey

It's important that some things you read to your students come from books by minority authors.

First Grade

Chrysanthemum by Kevin Henkes

Owen by Kevin Henkes

Don't Fidget a Feather! by Erica Silverman

Blackberries in the Dark by Mavis Jukes

The Bossy Gallifo by Lucia Gonzalez

Just Us Women by Jeannette Caines

Green Eggs and Ham by Dr. Seuss

Lyle, Lyle, Crocodile by Bernard Waber

Millions of Cats by Wanda Gag

The Mysterious Tadpole by Steven Kellogg

I have provided titles of several books written by authors from other cultures for each grade level.

Second Grade

Piggie Pie! by Margie Palatini

Thunder Cake by Patricia Polacco

Cinderella's Rat by Susan Meddaugh

Rabbit Hill by Robert Lawson

The Patchwork Quilt by Valerie Flournoy

The Mouse and the Motorcyle by Beverly Cleary

Hog Eye by Susan Meddaugh

Ribsy by Beverly Cleary

Mirandy and Brother Wind by Patricia McKissack

Third grade

Fly, Homer, Fly by Bill Peet

Little House in the Big Woods by Laura Ingalls Wilder

Charlotte's Web by E. B. White

Justin and the Best Biscuits in the World
   by Mildred P. Walter

James and the Giant Peach by Roald Dahl

Zella, Zach, and Zodiac by Bill Peet

Ramona by Beverly Cleary

Lafcadio, the Lion Who Shot Back by Shel Silverstein

The Velveteen Rabbit by Margery Williams Bianco

Fourth Grade

Jennifer Murdley's Toad by Bruce Coville

Wilma Unlimited by Kathleen Krull

The Lion, the Witch, and the Wardrobe by C. S. Lewis

Island of the Blue Dolphins by Scott O'Dell

Grey Cloud by Charlotte Graeber

Off and Running by Gary Soto

Otis Spofford by Beverly Cleary

The Ghost-Eye Tree by Bill Martin, Jr.

The Case of the Goblin Pearls by Laurence Yep

Stuart Little by E. B. White

Fifth Grade

Beauty by Bill Wallace

Martin's Mice by Dick King-Smith

Roll of Thunder, Hear My Cry by Mildred Taylor

I Thought My Soul Would Rise and Fly by Joyce Hansen

King of the Wind by Marguerite Henry

Where the Lilies Bloom by Vera Cleaver

The Star Fisher by Lawrence Yep

My Side of the Mountain by Jean Craighead George

Confessions of a Prime Time Kid by Mark Harris

The Trumpet of the Swan by E. B. White

I Thought My Soul Would Rise and Fly, by Hansen, was designated a Coretta Scott King Honor Award book.

Sixth Grade

The True Confessions of Charlotte Doyle by Avi

The Giver by Lois Lowry

The Call of the Wild by Jack London

Path of the Pale Horse by Paul Fleischman

Thank You, Jackie Robinson by Barbara Cohen

Sing Down the Moon by Scott O'Dell

Call It Courage by Armstrong Sperry

The Watsons Go to Birmingham – 1963
   by Christopher Paul Curtis

Long After Midnight by Ray Bradbury

Darnell Rock Reporting by Walter Dean Myers

Keep Parents Informed

Parents may well be your best resource for classroom help and it's very important to make them feel part of your overall team. An excellent way to do this is through frequent letters, memos and phone calls. A comprehensive letter at the beginning of the year will be welcomed by parents who want to know what kind of teacher you are.

Homework each night:

• Kindergarten—15 minutes

• Primary—30 minutes

• Intermediate—45 minutes

A veteran teacher suggests the following items be covered:

- Give the date for Back-to-School Night.

- Tell parents exactly which day your weekly letter will be sent home.

- Explain what will be included, such as a story to be read in the reader and lists of vocabulary words, spelling words and math facts for youngsters to study for the weekly tests.

- Suggest homework rules, depending upon your district and grade level, such as students to read aloud to an adult each night and study math facts and spelling words.

- List dismissal times for the first week of school and the regular dismissal time if different.

- List items children need to bring to school such as pencils, crayons and erasers, if needed.

- Urge parents to be sure their children wear sturdy shoes to school, not party shoes.

- List days and times when you would welcome parents in the classroom to help or to visit.

- Ask for help when going on field trips, holding bake sales and during classroom parties.

Teaching can often be a stress-filled job. Every teacher should have access to a Jacuzzi.™

Students Go Home

When your students are dismissed to go home, be sure they have your information letter in hand, in lunch boxes or pinned to a garment of the youngest children.

5

First Week

Yesterday, the first day of school, Ted had 26 students plus four "no-shows" on his fourth-grade class list. He knows some of these "no-shows" may appear today and he wants to be prepared in case they arrive while he's busy teaching.

Ted, a substitute, arrived at school early to check that the four empty desks had everything ready with a pencil, eraser, scissors and textbooks inside.

After just one day, Ted's concerned about the class. He can already tell that several children will be behavior problems. In response, he plans to move three desks to separate these students.

Before the class arrives, he'll write the day's schedule on the chalkboard. He'll also list the procedures to follow when going out to recess. This schedule will serve as a reminder of recess and lunch breaks and cut down on questions.

Assign a child to keep an empty desk equipped for the arrival of any new student.

TEACHER TIP: *Rather than spend time each morning writing out a daily schedule, consider using a large piece of tagboard and writing each subject followed by a line. Then laminate the board for years of service. At the end of each day, erase the assignments and write the new ones on the subject lines.*

Students who misbehave or talk constantly can drain your energy. Treat yourself to a full body massage monthly to relieve stress.

Just as he did yesterday, Ted has planned short lessons followed by breaks for discussions of classroom rules and procedures. He purposely has selected lessons that the entire group can enjoy and do successfully. He wants all the students to feel confident and know they can do well.

Since he doesn't know the children's abilities yet, he'll teach to the entire class. By next week, when he has more information on each student, he'll begin to work with small groups. Ted's lesson plans are over-prepared today because he wants to leave as little time as possible for behavior problems to develop.

Have your own rules and procedures in mind before the opening day of school.

He arranged the desks into learning groups and will collaborate with the class on rules and procedures beginning the first day.

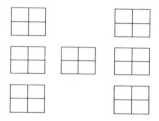

Yesterday, before leaving school, he placed all the papers for today's lessons in order along one side of a long table placed up front and the center of the room.

Remember the saying, "Without a vision, people perish!"

Since reading groups have not yet been established, Ted has saved copies of the "Weekly Reader" to use during the reading period. He'll read one of the major stories with the class, then assign questions and crossword puzzles as seatwork.

As he gives the room a final check before going to the faculty room for a cup of coffee, he's interrupted by a knock at the door. A new student greets him and hands him a yellow admit slip. The boy explains, "We just moved here yesterday." Ted notes that the student is from out-of-state.

He'll need to give the youngster an informal reading test to find his reading level, since he came without any school records.

A teacher *must* be flexible.

Ted's story is true; only his name has been changed. He substituted in a fourth-grade class for nearly a month until a teacher with more seniority was hired. However, Ted did an outstanding job in getting the class started, rules established and Class Meetings begun, which carried over when the new teacher entered the classroom.

♣ HINT: If you're hired to sub at the beginning of the year, try, as Ted did, to get the class organized quickly, get all testing done and lay the foundation for a successful school year, even if you know you won't be the permanent teacher. Your early efforts will pay off for the students, as well as the new teacher, all through the school year. And your efforts can earn you a good reference as they did for Ted.

Information Card

In order to help place students at proper levels in reading and math at the beginning of the year, many school districts require an End-of-the-Year Information Card on each student. If you use such a card, here's what needs to appear on it.

- Indicate current reader, reading test grade and page number.
- List math book, test grade and page number.
- You may also list behavior problems and any need to separate the student from another youngster.

Early/Late Reading

Some school districts use the early/late reading program. If your district does, it's often helpful to divide the class right down the middle. Have the students needing the most help come in the morning when they're more awake and interested and you're fresh.

By having your good readers stay in the afternoon, you may have fewer behavior problems. You'll leave school happy and looking forward to coming back the next day.

Reading is such a vital skill that you must do what's best for each student.

What if parents want a child in a particular reading group? Meet with or call the parents and collaborate on what would be best for the student. You need to be diplomatic when parents ask you to put their child in a higher reader or a different reading group. Explain that the child will achieve best in the reader, or group, you have assigned unless there's a good reason for changing.

Total-Class Reading Program

When all students come to school at the same time, there are several ways to teach reading.

- Test and divide the class into no more than three or four reading groups. One group might play reading games, another picks partners who read to each other, a third group works on phonics paperwork and a fourth, emphasizing good handwriting, does a book report. They could trade activities after a period of time. Check your teacher's edition for guidelines.

- Alternate teacher-directed reading with one of the above groups while the other groups do seatwork. Many teachers work directly with two groups each day.

♣ HINT: Read your teacher's manual for help in setting up reading groups. Also, for additional help, attend all workshops based upon your reading series.

- Join with other teachers in an exchange program where students reading on one level go to another teacher. Some teachers enjoy the exchange and others don't. You'll need to work this out at your own school.

- If you have a junior or senior high school nearby, ask for helpers during reading.

- Find parent volunteers or retired people in the community who are willing to come in on a regular basis to help during this class.

- When a reading specialist is available and you have students with reading problems, ask for help at once. Don't wait, as it takes time to file the paperwork, have the child tested and get on the specialist's schedule.

- While you instruct one group, schedule another group for reading programs on classroom computers, when available. Many reading series come with software lessons for the computer.

- Ask your principal to provide an aide during reading. (And, longer if possible!)

Readers Go Home

In order to be good readers, students must read. Each night, insist your students take their readers home. One way to keep track of these books is to have all students place their reading books on top of their desks when they arrive in the morning. Write the names of those who don't on sticky notes and place on your lesson plans, for this indicates either they left the book at home or the reader is lost. Remind these students before going home to look for the book that night.

Don't let students call home for parents to drive books to school. Help students develop responsibility for their school materials.

Suggestions for First-Week Reading Activities

Students at most grade levels enjoy playing bingo. Use this interest during the first week, both as a review of skills and a fun activity done in short increments of time. Numerous good variations can be purchased at a teacher's bookstore or ordered through an educational materials catalog.

Kindergarten

Alphabet Bingo™

- Each playing-card square features an upper-case letter and its lower-case partner for alphabet recognition. Available in sets of 36.

Primary

Vowel Bingo™

- Cards 1-18 have single-syllable words. Cards 19-36 have single- and multiple-syllable words.
- Students can identify over 280 different labeled pictures with the consonants, *br* and *st* blends, and *ch*, *sh*, *th* and *wh* digraphs. Available in sets of 36.

Intermediate

USA Bingo™

Have a student assigned to see that all games and puzzles are complete. Missing parts create numerous problems. Get rid of incomplete games.

- Four different game categories include states and capitals, postal abbreviations, state nicknames, slogans and trivia teasers. Available in sets of 36.

Primary and intermediate students thoroughly enjoy doing crossword puzzles which can be purchased at teacher bookstores. Students can do these alone, with a partner or make their own.

A good way to teach listening skills is to take your students outdoors and have each pick a partner. Then tell them to listen carefully as you give instructions.

 EXAMPLE: Say, "I want you and your partner to 1) count the number of fence posts around our playground, 2) count the number of red bikes in the bike racks and, 3) count the number of trees on our school grounds. You are to report back to me when you hear me blow the whistle twice. You'll have eight minutes. Start now!"

Prepare for Recess

Be considerate of others, and don't open your door and let your students fly outside for recess or to the cafeteria. Not only can they get hurt but the noise distracts other classes.

You need to continue to teach rules and procedures each day in the classroom. When doing this, you must:

- Explain what you want your students to do. If possible, write out the directions ahead of time and review them orally just prior to usage.
- Select a small group of students to demonstrate the rule or procedure.
- If they make a mistake, explain what they do right. Praise and repeat the practice. The few who do it wrong will correct themselves.

Here is a good example to use for teaching procedures. As a teacher, you'll spend a great deal of time moving students from the classroom to the cafeteria, library and playground.

During the first month of school, have your students role play how to move from place-to-place efficiently.

Have four students line up in the classroom as models. Show them how far apart they should stand so as not to step on or bump the student in front of them.

Ask the students to then walk slowly across the floor so all can see how the line moves. Remind the youngsters that one student will lead the others and you'll be at the end of the line.

●◆ NOTE: Before the class leaves the room, tell students where to go and which route to take.

It's usually best to have your students walk in short segments from the classroom to, for example, the library. Ask them to pause when they get to room six and wait for you to say "go." Then they walk on to room seven and pause and wait for your "go" and move on to the library.

Remember when giving instructions that you have both visual and auditory learners in your classroom. By providing the visual steps and orally repeating them, you can help *all* your students understand what you want them to do.

The following is an example of what you can write on the chalkboard or on a handout to give students to prepare for recess.

- Clear off your desk and put everything away.
- Stand up.
- Push your chair under your desk.
- Walk quietly, without talking, to the back of the room.
- At my signal, walk quietly outside to the playground.
- The teacher will be observing at the end of the line.

♣ HINT: Practice the directions until *everyone* gets them right. *Accept no less.*

If some students have a problem following your teaching of rules and procedures, check to be sure all understand what they're to do. It could be that you need to reteach and role play a specific rule or procedure.

Responsibility for Learning

Throughout the entire year you must tell your students about the importance of learning. You need to help them understand how learning benefits them.

- Talk with your students about the necessity of being able to read. Explain that before they can drive a car, they must read and study the driver's manual in order to pass the test.
- When teaching math, explain with visuals why students must learn the basic facts so they can make change, keep a checkbook and purchase food.
- Talk about the importance of acting properly within the classroom community. Then explain how obtaining a good job and getting along with friends and family are much easier when we know how to behave.

The end of the line is where the "action" usually takes place. Be there to cut down on any start of misbehavior.

How to line up and go out to recess is an ideal lesson to teach rules and procedures.

Have all students choral read directions (read in unison) with you at the snap of your fingers.

Some students fuss about many things as a way to get attention.

- Discuss the necessity of being able to write a complete sentence and a memo or a business letter in order to succeed in the workplace.

Future wages Show how it's also a *big loss* financially for a student to fool around in school and not graduate from high school. Why?

Write on the chalkboard or overhead the sum $212,000. Explain that on average, a high-school dropout will make 212,000 fewer dollars over a lifetime than someone who stays in high school and graduates.

Then write $800,000 on the board. Again tell your students that this is the amount of financial loss they'll suffer in their lifetime if they drop out of college. This survey was done by the Educational Testing Service.

TEACHER TIP: *It's vital that we in elementary school make the time to help our students understand why they come to school. Statistics indicate the majority of young people who drop out have no idea why they were in school. You can change this lack of direction by helping your students understand the importance of learning to read, doing math, writing well and getting along with others.*

Lunch Break

You should have set the timer to go off 5-7 minutes before lunch break, allowing time to again role play how to walk to the cafeteria.

Repeat the morning recess procedure for teaching students to put their things away, stand up, push chairs under their desks and follow instructions to line up. This time remind them to bring their lunches or lunch money.

Ask students how much money people earn at minimum wages. Ask how many with college degrees work for that amount. Why not?

As previously indicated, line up the class by small groups to reduce noise, confusion and pushing in line.

T.N.T. = Talk and Talk

With many students working in groups, talking is important in peer coaching, group interaction and movement by students around the room.

Make students aware of voice volume. Show them by example and have students role play.

- Number-one voice is a soft, conversational voice.
- Number-two voice is for giving oral reports.
- Number-three voice is a playground voice—loud!

Instead of your talking all the time, use finger signs when possible. Hold up one finger to remind a loud student of a soft classroom voice. Raise two fingers for an oral-report voice and three when outside and a student's normal voice can't be heard.

Sing Along with Me

As a break from the first week's routine of teaching rules and procedures, plan short breaks for singing. You may sing without accompaniment or use a CD, cassette tape or recorder. Students enjoy lively songs.

Kindergarten

- Eensie Weensie Spider
- It's a Small World
- Pop Goes the Weasel

Before lunch on day two, have two students role play how it feels to get to the cafeteria without a lunch or money. You might have one role play how *you* feel when you must return to the classroom with forgetful students.

Before going to assemblies discuss how to behave and not talk at these meetings. Perhaps certain "pilot lights" shouldn't be in the same group, as they "ignite" each other.

Primary

- This Old Man
- Old MacDonald
- Row, Row, Row Your Boat

Intermediate

- I've Been Working on the Railroad
- This Land Is Your Land
- America the Beautiful

T.G.I.F

Whether you're a substitute or a regular classroom teacher, you've made it through the first, and one of the most important, weeks in the school year. You've taught rules and procedures to your students, told them how important school is and finished on a happy note by singing lively songs. Congratulations!

6

First Month: Policies and Procedures

Seventember is *the* critical month in teaching. The rules, procedures and classroom management system you establish now are crucial to your classroom success for the rest of the year.

Let's briefly review what you did the first week:

- You established a reason for coming to school.
- You taught lessons to the total class.
- You presented short assignments.
- You planned for brief periods of instruction of rules and procedures in the classroom.
- You began to select rules with students' input to help reach the goal.

> **R-e-p-e-a-t**

Now you'll narrow your approach. You will:

- Continue to review classroom rules and procedures.
- Develop student accountability for doing their work.

To teach rules:
- Repeat.
- Repeat.
- Repeat.

- Establish classroom policies about homework, class work and behavior.

Whether you're a new teacher or a veteran, you must KNOW and FEEL, "I can handle these students. I'm the adult and they're the children."

For most teachers this means saying to themselves, " I'm a great teacher! I look my students in the eye each morning as I greet them." A warm smile also helps you begin each day on a positive note.

You and you alone must decide how you'll approach your students. Never forget, however, that you're the role model in the classroom.

Keep parents informed Just as students must know what to expect in the classroom, parents also need to be informed. At the beginning of the year, many school districts send home some type of Parent Handbook which will normally include the following information:

- Arrival and dismissal times
- Behavior policy
- Absence policy
- PTA activities
- Room parents
- Homework policy
- Special school programs and teachers such as:

    - Bilingual teacher

    - Psychological services

    - Reading resource teacher

    - Speech teacher

If your classroom rules and policies aren't included, discuss them in one of your weekly newsletters. Suggest that parents keep them for the entire year.

Rules

During the first week you and your students began to select the rules for your classroom. By now they should be written clearly and posted where everyone can see them. Start using them.

For example, you're busy teaching reading to one group while the other students are doing seatwork. You see Dennis, in another group, throw his eraser at Brandon three desks away.

This is the time to walk over and look at Dennis. Use this time to quietly, yet firmly so all can hear you, talk to Dennis about rules and behavior. Let the problem behavior become a "teaching-behavior" lesson for the entire class.

TEACHER TIP: *Don't let behavior problems interfere with your recess or lunch break. Settle on a management system that doesn't keep you in the classroom during these times. You need this opportunity to go to the bathroom, pick up messages in the office and relax.*

Your rules should be:
• Short
• Relevant
• Respectful
• Clear about your basic expectations

Teach the rules Students need time to learn classroom rules and procedures. As you did the first week, allow a time each day to discuss the rules and go over procedures until you're certain each student understands what's expected. When new students enter, go over the rules and procedures once again. This is a natural time for a review for all students.

Be consistent One of the most difficult things to do every day of the teaching year is to be consistent about rules. But this is so important. Your pattern is established the first month.

Graphing

One visual way to help students grasp their responsibility in school is to draw graphs. See the example of the Tina/Susan graph here. Use this illustration or pick two other names.

With brightly colored projector pens, draw the outline of the graph. Put in days and dates at the bottom and numbers from 10 to 100 up the left side.

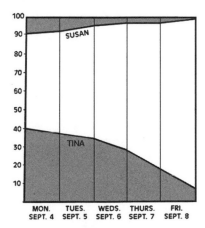

THE SUCCESS/FAILURE GRAPH

Tell the story, for example, about Tina. Explain that she was late the first two days of school and finished only part of her math assignment both days and received a poor grade. On the third day she didn't know her spelling words and on Thursday and Friday she was late and forgot her homework.

Explain that Tina forgets homework, can't find a pencil in her messy desk and fiddles around during class with a bracelet she's wearing.

On the other hand, Susan pays attention, does her homework and is interested in getting smarter this year so she can go on to the next grade.

As you tell the story, draw the lines for Tina and Susan as shown. Ask, "Which line do you choose?" Then call upon a student to explain to the class what the graph means to him or her. Continue to tell stories each day and, if needed, throughout the school year. Allow time for class discussion of this vital subject each day.

There's security in having a regular routine.

Teaching About Procedures

As a new teacher you may be surprised to learn you're the one stable person in a student's life. Veteran teachers know from first-hand experience that unfortunately, this is very true. In our rapidly changing American families, many students have little stability in their homes. These students will depend upon you not only as their teacher, but also as a friend and anchor in their chaotic lives.

CAUTION: At a time when many boys and girls desperately need hugs, holding and a pat on the back, you'll need to be careful. Lawsuits are escalating against teachers for hugging and touching children. The suits are aimed at both men and women but more often, at men. Be aware of this in your classroom.

You can be an anchor for your students.

A key to making students feel secure and safe is well-defined rules and procedures which give a solid, predictable structure to the classroom. You'll certainly need to dwell upon your rules and procedures the first month or longer, as needed.

An opening ceremony to begin each day can include any or all of the following:

- A good-morning greeting
- Saluting the flag
- Singing a song
- Taking attendance
- Taking lunch count
- Collecting milk and lunch money
- Collecting homework
- Mentioning the date
- Discussing the weather
- Holding an emergency Class Meeting if problems of a serious nature develop

Procedure for heading papers As soon as possible, provide a lesson for your students on how you want them to head their papers during the year. One method is described here.

Draw a large illustration of a sheet of paper on the chalkboard or overhead. Use your own name and write it in the upper right- or left-hand corner, as you choose. Under the name, clearly write the date and subject such as "Language."

Take a large sheet of your writing paper and write the same information on it. Walk slowly around the room so all can see your model.

Now have a student pass out paper; afterward, slowly lead the class through the correct writing of name, subject and date. Some will do this quickly while others will need more time. Teach the heading lesson for three or four days until you're sure all students understand what is expected.

TEACHER TIP: *Try a "reminder game" to help students get their names on their papers. Stand on your tiptoes and reach your hand up high. Tell the students, "Reach for the sky, then touch your name." With an exaggerated motion, zip your hand down with your index finger onto your name. It works!*

Some students have such sloppy handwriting it's difficult to read their names. You may wish to assign a number to each student to write and circle above his or her name. This will also make it easier for you to mark by number in your record book.

Turning in work It's important that your students know which work must be turned in to you, which held over to the next day for classroom grading and which is simply review. Make your expectations clear. Also, provide a special place for incoming work:

- In plastic color-coded bins
- Under a seashell on a table
- In subject-titled folders

One teacher calls the roll each morning and has each named student stand up and say, "Good morning, Mrs. Wilson. I've brought back my math and language papers and here they are." Students then bring the work to her.

Correcting work No matter which method you use, be consistent, grade as quickly as possible and return papers to students promptly. They need to see and correct their errors at once.

Studies indicate that students who hear, see or write a math fact 26 times have it for life. However, if they learn it incorrectly, such as 4 + 4 = 7, it can take literally hundreds of repetitions to correct such an error in the brain. *It is vital* that students do their work correctly the first time.

Teaching is a stressful occupation, partly because of the need to find a way to keep up with the daily chore of grading papers. Many teachers find it an overwhelming job. You must find an effective method which still leaves you a life outside the classroom. It may be asking an aide or parent to do some for you, paying a high school student to help or having your own students correct certain papers in the classroom.

One teacher, with the help of a parent, moves around the room correcting math papers as they're finished. The teacher and parent mark them in red pencil.

If a student has an "A" paper, he or she is handed a blue pencil and becomes a student helper. If questions should arise, the teacher can double-check the blue marks the student helper made on a fellow student's paper.

Some teachers ask for an additional teacher's edition of the textbook for student use. They make a special book cover marked

---

After 26 exposures to a fact, your students have it for life.

"Correcting Book." A correcting monitor is assigned (or elected) once a week. The student corrector sits at a table and corrects papers. The rule is that no more than three students can be in line at any one time, to prevent talking or pushing.

Student Accountability

Allow students to take responsibility for themselves by letting them know that specific work is due each day and where to put completed work so it can be corrected and returned as soon as possible. When they fail to turn it in, you'll hear many silly stories. Try to keep a straight face.

TEACHER TIP: *During the first month of school, establish a homework buddy system. Pair off students who live near each other. When one is absent, the other takes the buddy's work to him or her and returns completed work.*

Tall tales of woe:
• "My baby sister ate my math."
• "My dad threw away my spelling."
• "My mom washed my science report."

Passing out and collecting materials

▪ Do as quickly as possible to keep students from getting restless.

▪ Put a student in charge of passing out papers and collecting them.

▪ When passing out numerous items (such as during art), have a lesson or activity to keep students occupied.

Incomplete work
Particularly during the first month of school, you must let your students know your policy regarding incomplete work. Ask yourself several questions about accepting work not finished:

▪ Will I expect most work to be completed in class?

▪ When work is not completed in class, when will it be done?

▪ If turned in unfinished, will I return the paper to the student to complete? If so, how will I keep track of this?

▪ When students finally complete overdue assignments, where will they turn in the work? In a special basket or where I collect regular work?

When considering accepting incomplete work, ask yourself, "Am I helping this student prepare for the workplace?"

- If I accept incomplete work, how much will I deduct from the total grade?
- If I have students with special needs, such as bilingual children with reading and language problems, should I expect them to complete as much work as others in the classroom?
- How can I best motivate my students to complete their work?

Teacher accountability for students' incomplete work If you're getting a lot of incomplete or inaccurate work in your classroom, there may be a problem in your presentation. You'll want to ask yourself these questions:

- Do my students understand what I expect from them regarding written lessons?
- Did I remember to show them a sample of the work and did I allow enough time for answering questions before they began the assignment?
- Did I give clear instructions before they began the lesson?

 REMEMBER: As your students have specific responsibilities to you, you in turn are responsible for providing clear, concise and understandable directions to them.

Teacher and students must share learning responsibilities.

Unfinished assignments and behavior problems
Sometimes you may still be faced with students who don't finish assignments—and present behavior problems besides. Again, you must act promptly. Speak to the child, warning that if this behavior continues, you'll need to conference with the child and parents. You may also need to place the student on a daily contract to be sure all work is completed as assigned and/or that behavior will be improved.

A contract can be as simple as a 3x5 card with the child's name and date at the top and your signature and a brief comment. If parents are brought in, the child should sit in on the conference and must take part and suggest ways to overcome his or her problem.

Examples of special problems Not all students fit into the same mold. Some work well in groups. Others don't. In order to run an efficient classroom, you must try to meet these individual needs. Tony, for instance, was a behavior problem from the time he entered fourth grade. He frequently yelled out, bothered those around him and seldom turned in his work on time. One day as his teacher was considering a contract, he surprised her by asking, "Can I move my desk over in that corner and sit by myself? I just want to be alone."

She agreed and helped Tony move his desk. He stayed in that corner, by his own choice, for the remainder of the year and both his grades and behavior improved.

TEACHER TIP: *Provide a "Retreat" place for your students. This could be a desk in a quiet corner; a large cardboard refrigerator box with the top couple of feet removed, a door cut into one side and a desk inside; or a large pillow where a student can go to be alone. This special spot may be used by a student for only five minutes or as long as needed.*

Other problems can't be so easily solved. Lewis, one of my third graders, had signed a contract to improve his behavior and complete his schoolwork. His *new* behavior lasted two days.

On day three, he trashed the bathroom. Quietly, I told him the custodian had agreed to oversee his cleanup project. He was given the choice of who would inspect when he finished—the custodian, the yard teacher or myself.

While washing walls, hauling out trash and scrubbing the floor, he learned a lot about being a responsible and respectful person.

NOTE: I didn't yell at him or call his parents. I simply handed him a broom and dustpan, and my brief talk with him about responsibility was loud enough to be overheard by his fellow students. The elbow-grease lesson empowered Lewis more than any parents' or principal's input ever would have. It also made a good class learning/teaching experience.

Sometimes a fellow just needs to be alone.

Not all class learning experiences are the result of problem behavior. Some are necessary because of ordinary, everyday activities in the classroom.

Cleaning out desks at regular intervals is vital to help students stay organized and you should explain why. Also, particularly after an art lesson, it's important to clean desktops of glue, crayon marks and drops of paint.

One effective way to do this is to have your students use men's instant shaving cream. It not only does a terrific clean-up job, but also makes the room smell nice afterward!

Much of your success for the school year depends upon setting up fair and reasonable rules and procedures early and having your students follow them consistently throughout the year. If you are confident, prepared and flexible, it will help demonstrate that you are a capable and concerned teacher.

7

First Month: Motivating Your Students

Motivation

It's sad but true; you *cannot make* your students learn. You can present the class with brightly colored math books, clean sheets of paper and use your flashiest pens on the overhead projector while teaching, yet your students may show little or no interest in learning.

But don't give up. You can arrange your classroom and your teaching units to motivate your students to learn.

Getting smarter "As teachers, we face a problem," says Dr. David Berliner at Arizona State University. "Most teachers come from the middle class where an education is a primary goal. In our rapidly changing society we are dealing with culturally different groups of students. Many parents from the lower class view school as a place of failure and frustration. They actually fear school. Yet as teachers, we must continue to find ways to get these parents into our classrooms so we can join together in educating their children."

My students need
to know:
• I care.
• I believe in them.
• I accept them.

From the very beginning of the year, discuss cooperatively with the class the importance of learning. Talk as a group about having only one body and mind and why not take a smart body and mind through life.

Caring It's critical that your students know you accept them, care about them and believe in them. This can have a major life-long impact upon their attitude toward school and learning. From the first day say things like, "I *expect* my students will be the best-behaved class in the cafeteria today." Use your power of expectation to empower your students to know they can achieve and you *expect* they will. They will tune in to this. And when they achieve, give praise and a big smile and say, "I knew you could."

Marva Collins, an outstanding Chicago educator, tells her students, "You are too bright for me to let you fail." Her positive talk over the years has changed hundreds of students from "I can'ts" to "I cans!"

Marva Collins:
• Determination
• Vision
• Positive talk

In her book, *Marva Collins' Way*, a "must read" for every teacher, she details her determination, vision and positive belief in children. More positive statements from her book include:

- "You are the best and brightest children in the world and there is nothing you can't do."

- "You must decide for yourself what you want to do here. You have the right to learn. You also have the right to fail, if you choose."

- "No one is going to hand you anything on a platter, not in this classroom. Not in this life. You determine what you will be, what you will make of yourselves. I am here to help you, but you must help me to do that. You can ALL win if you do not spend too much time trying to fail."

Teacher enthusiasm "Bored teachers produce bored students," says one educator. Use positive ways to motivate your students to want to learn, get smart and go on to the next grade.

Enthusiastic teacher =
Enthusiastic students.

Bored teacher =
Bored students.

When you're enthusiastic, your students will pay better attention and become excited about school.

Variety Since students become bored listening to a teacher who drones on and on, variety is a key to maintaining enthusiasm. Move around, convey sincere interest in the subject and be excited about the lesson.

Place your students into groups. Provide an opportunity for your boys and girls to work together on a variety of units such as science, language and social studies.

❧ NOTE: Remember, you're competing with a steady diet of computer games, the Internet, videos, CDs and rapid-fire television. To keep your students' interest, you must demonstrate that the lesson has more value for them than pure entertainment.

This interest can be gained by several logical steps:

- Give a purpose for the lesson by showing students how the information can serve them.
- Start with the familiar and move to the unfamiliar by "hooking" the known to the unknown.

- Use a lesson plan to guide your students on a step-by-step progression toward the learning goal.
- Point out reasonable relationships and then compare and contrast.
- Finally, at the end of the lesson and again at the end of the day, remind students what they have learned and how it will help them in their own lives.

Sponges In an average day, many precious learning moments are lost while waiting for the bell to ring, changing from one subject to another or waiting to go home. These minutes can be used for oral work which we call "sponges." Tiny bits and pieces of knowledge can be squeezed into these teaching moments.

There are numerous kinds of sponges you might toss out to your class as they are lined up and waiting to go outside:

- What city in our state has the most syllables in its name?
- Which month of the year has the most syllables? Which car? Which food?
- Spell this week's spelling words.
- Sing several songs.
- Count to 100 by twos. Fives. Tens.
- Say the sevens tables in multiplication. Eights. Nines.
- Name the main character in the book I'm reading aloud to you this week. The setting? Author? Illustrator?

Sponge:
A bit of knowledge squeezed into an odd moment.

"Think-time"
• Pretend.
• Imagine.
• What if?
• Consider.
• Think about...

Encourage success "Success or lack of success in a school subject eventually is a major force in determining how the student feels about the subject and his or her desire to know more about that subject," says Dr. B. S. Bloom, Chicago educator.

Generally, motivated students have a much more positive concept of self, can use language well to express themselves and are open to ideas. Unmotivated students are just the opposite. Often it's up to you to help each student want to learn and succeed. Some effective ideas are:

- Use cross-age tutors. They could, for example, be students from your intermediate grades, from a nearby junior high or a local high school.

- Ask parents with particular skills to present special lessons. One student's mother was a musician and each week brought her guitar to teach music.

- Plan exciting field trips to either introduce or be a grand finale to a new unit.

- Use charts to illustrate the number of library books read.

- Display good work on your bulletin board.

How students learn Students are motivated to learn either by "extrinsic" (outside) motivators or "intrinsic" (inside) ones.

An example of extrinsic motivation might be a spelling test on Friday. The teacher states the test will be a big review of the words given in the past month. A reluctant learner might be motivated by *pressure* to study the words. Also, impending parent conferences or report cards may create sufficient extrinsic pressure to get the student going.

Some students are motivated intrinsically simply by the "good feelings" which come when an oral report is completed, a good book finished or a science experiment has succeeded.

Remember your students will respond and be motivated in different ways. You *must* become aware of the best way to reach each child.

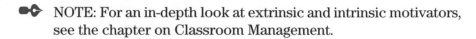 NOTE: For an in-depth look at extrinsic and intrinsic motivators, see the chapter on Classroom Management.

Include all students in class discussions It's important that all students participate in class discussions. That means both boys and girls, more-reserved students and those who are outgoing. Often, we tend to call upon students who we feel will know the answer.

TEACHER TIP: *Choose your method for having your students respond to questions. Will they raise their hands? Do a "thumbs up" and "down" for yes and no answers? One idea that works well in getting all students involved in discussions is to print each student's name on a wooden popsicle stick. Place them in a coffee cup on your desk. Draw a stick each time and after calling upon that student, replace the stick so no one is "off the hook." Always look for something right in an answer to an oral question.*

Feedback Feedback is an important component of motivation. Looking for something correct about students' answers or work helps keep them enthusiastic and eager to please you, their teacher.

After a history test you could say, "You did a great job on this test. I marked only one paragraph. Please check these two dates and return your paper to me." You've told your student he or she was successful on the test as well as what else needs to be done.

If a student failed the history test, you might want to hold a "one-on-one" in the back of the room, or before or after school. You could talk about how long he or she studied for the test. Provide some suggestions on how the student could better prepare; then let him or her restudy and retake the test.

If a number of students have a problem passing a test, it may be a sign of insufficient instruction. Review the questions with the whole class and discuss each one again. Perhaps they weren't clear on what information would be tested or the questions were confusing.

In this type of situation, I've often found it helpful for all youngsters if I use the overhead projector to review missed questions with the total class.

Place an overlay on the overhead to show the most-missed questions. Then use bright, colorful pens to underline, circle and star specific information wherever needed within each question.

Have your students take out their crayons (or colored pencils) and similarly mark their returned test papers while following your example. Not only do you help students who missed certain questions, but you're also reteaching the information for all students.

I'd also suggest you remind your class again of the importance of getting plenty of sleep before a test and eating a nutritious breakfast before leaving for school. Studies indicate that students following this routine often make higher test grades.

Also vital to success is a final reminder to your students that they not wait until the night before to study for a test. They must begin preparation several days before.

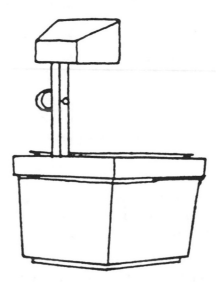

High expectations Always remember the importance of motivation. Studies indicate that successful schools have high expectations for their students. As teachers, we must *expect* that all our students will learn and we must help them achieve this goal.

There are many things in your students' lives you can do nothing about such as home environment, degree of parental help and concern, money or lack of it, single-parent home or a strong family unit. But *you can* help each student find his or her own best way to learn and to become successful in school.

8

First Month: Introduction of Lessons

During the first two weeks of school, you have presented short lessons followed by brief reviews of classroom rules and procedures.

For some classes, two weeks is long enough to teach rules, but for classes with many behavior problems, you might need to spend the entire first month reinforcing the rules. You alone can determine when it's time to move on. By the end of the month, however, you should begin to move into longer lessons, units and homework assignments. You'll also move from a "total-room focus" to smaller groups.

Students need to:
- Be responsible.
- Be self-directed.
- Stay motivated.

Reading

By the second week of school, you should have an idea of reading levels for each child from the previous year's information cards, from testing included in your reading series or your own testing of the child.

The teacher's edition book of your reading series will tell in the opening pages how to teach the program. A number of reading programs feature learning units which may focus on concepts from science and social studies.

Home input is vital More and more educators are reaching out to parents for help at home. This is especially important in reading. Some series, in order to reach all parents, provide sample letters in both English and Spanish so you can send either to parents.

Activity sheets are often provided for parents and children to complete together, along with a list of good books for families to share at home.

Reading in the classroom is taught through poetry, realistic fiction, historical fiction and world-wide literature.

Students need to know:

- How to gain information
- How to evaluate it
- How to adapt it

No longer is reading taught to students from just one book. Usually several books are used. Other activities to develop reading skills include spelling; writing; editing on computers; and listening to stories on tapes, CDs and those read aloud at school or home. As a bonus, stories teach children how to live in their world.

TEACHER TIP: *As a new teacher, be careful about exchanging students. If you send two students to another room, tell the receiving teacher that you'll accept only two students reading on a level you'll be teaching. Problems can arise when some teachers take advantage of others.*

Writing enhances reading It's important that students write if they're to read well. You can help encourage them to become writers:

- Have your students keep a journal and write in it each day.
- After students read a story, have them write a summary.

- Provide a CD or cassette tape player with stories for students to listen to at a learning center.
- Encourage your students to make greeting cards.

♣ HINT: Read a story on tape to which your students can listen

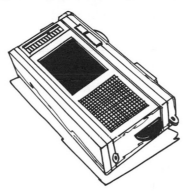

during their free time. Speak in a dramatic voice such as a king giving a command or a mother cooing to her baby.

Use a computer to help your students become involved in the writing process. Teach the youngsters to prewrite, draft, revise, proofread and publish. Afterward allow time for them to share what they've written.

Make your own stories on tape. Story ideas:
- Adapt from a book.
- Tell an original story.
- Tape a true story.

We must teach our students "how to learn."

Mathematics

Kindergarten A good book to have in your classroom is *Mathematics Their Way* by Mary Baratta-Lorton. You can use the skills depicted to assess the ability level of your kindergartners.

Many math programs come with manipulatives. Spend the early days of school encouraging your students to explore shapes, colors and sizes.

Consider having your students clap and count with you each day. This joyful experience leads to confidence with numbers.

Not all your students may know their own telephone numbers. Set up a center with an old telephone and a numberline glued to the table. Here they can practice dialing their home numbers.

Primary Most primary students can use the written test which comes with the math series. However, it's also important for you to observe and interview to discover what a child knows. For example, after testing you could ask a third grader to explain place value, how to subtract with borrowing and how to do a few multiplication facts to be sure the process is understood.

During the first month of school, primary students also need time to explore math manipulatives. This can be done as a group or individually at a math center.

Primary students should write reports about what they are doing in math. Set aside time when your students can think and then write about what they've learned.

Intermediate Students in grades four through six should be pretested at their grade level and again interviewed. For example, you could ask a sixth grader about fractions, decimals and division. This way you'll not only have a written inventory but the verbal account as well.

Intermediate students benefit from the use of manipulatives such as pattern blocks, geoboards, dice, protractors, playing cards and dominoes as part of their math program. Some publishers now provide manipulatives in the teacher's package.

After a lesson, allow time for your students to write about what they've been doing.

Intermediates enjoy estimating. A jar of beans, washers or buttons is a good place to begin. An outside activity could be estimating the number of cars in the parking lot and number of local birds huddled on the school grounds.

If your school's teachers exchange math students, be sure you take only your fair share of low-math children. Also, if you're given the lower-math students one year, ask to have the high group the following year.

> **TEACHER TIP:** *Consider carefully before exchanging math students if it would result in one large, low group for you. As an example, one teacher had 34 of the lowest math students one year. As expected, such a group was filled with behavior problems. Sadly, the message to the students was, "You're not smart and that's why you're in this group."*

Taking students outside for a math lesson energizes them. Change is helpful for teacher and students.

Cooperative Groups, 1-6

A cooperative-group room is one where students work together, usually with several students in each group. These can be changed every month or so.

Each cluster should consist of high-, average- and low-achieving students with a mix of gender and race, as well.

●← NOTE: Groups can be effective when using themes in the classroom. Here the class usually studies one theme for a period of time. One month students may learn about the "Indians of the West." Each group may study one tribe. Members of the group would be chosen to research the history, food-gathering methods and family units.

When studying in groups, students bond together, peer teaching takes place and the cluster works for the whole instead of competing against each other.

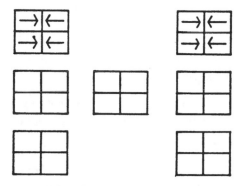

Classroom arrangement If this is your first time to use groups in your class, you must spend time preparing your students for the change. Talk about what will happen and how the desks will be placed and how clusters will be formed. This needs to be a discussion between teacher and students. You might also want to draw a sample group of desks on the chalkboard or overhead. Rules regarding noise, movement in and out of the group for materials, and who'll be the leader in each cluster need to be discussed in detail before beginning.

One example is shown here of a desk arrangement for a group lesson.

If you usually use another arrangement, have your students move their desks together into groups, one group at a time, just before lunch or recess. This will make it easier to launch the new arrangement quietly when you return to the classroom.

You may decide to use groups as a way for students to discuss math projects and make the larger connections between math and science, social studies, art and literature. This helps students communicate their ideas to others whether in the primary or intermediate grades.

For more information on forming groups, see the chapter on Classroom Management.

Say to auditory learners:
• Describe.
• Discuss.
• Explain.
• Listen.

Ask visual learners to:
• See.
• Picture.
• Watch.
• Visualize.

When giving directions to kinesthetic learners, you need to look directly at them and touch their shoulders as you speak. Be sure you have their full attention before you begin.

 HINT: When teaching reading, math or rules and procedures in your room, you must always keep in mind that you'll have a variety of learning-preference students. You'll have auditory and visual learners and also kinesthetic learners.

You may not always know which students are visual, auditory or kinesthetic (this is a small number). For this reason, it's wise to give assignments both verbally and written on the board for your visual learners.

Learning centers These centers can be used by a few students at a time. If studying counting, for example, you could set up a math center with cubes, marbles or popsicle sticks for counting. For reading, a small table could be used as a listening center where students plug into a cassette, listen and follow along with the book.

A center can be arranged on a desk top, at a table in the back of the room or at the side of the room if space is available.

 TEACHER TIP: *Never begin a new method of teaching without adequate preparation. Build in success for yourself. Take a class or workshop on the method, or ask a mentor teacher to help you get started. Make detailed plans.*

End of First Month of Teaching

As you move into the second month, you should be teaching reading and math for full periods. You might also be starting a science unit. You need to be aware of how many minutes your district expects for various subjects each week.

In addition, you must continue to motivate your students to learn each subject. Here are some extra ideas for each area of study.

Reading While you're working with one reading group, if you group, the rest of the class does seatwork. When finished, they could go to a center or stay at their desks and design a crossword puzzle, using either the vocabulary words from their story or the week's spelling words.

 HINT: If you have a computer, software is available to make vocabulary and spelling words into crossword puzzles.

Other students enjoy illustrating stories and creating book covers and small books for younger siblings.

Math Use the following idea for five minutes before beginning the math lesson. Cut 3x5 cards into squares about 2x2 inches. With a hole punch, make holes like the dots on a set of dominoes.

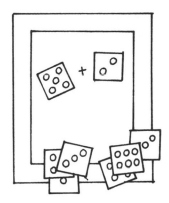

Reinforce math facts by taking two of the squares with holes and placing them on your darkened projector. With your pen, draw a "+," "-" or "x" between the squares. Tell the class you'll turn on the projector for only 5 seconds and they must be ready to give you back the complete fact orally.

Science Plan a unit on trees. To introduce your class to the unit, show slides or pictures of trees and leaves and insects which live on them. At the end of the first week, take your students on a walking field trip to a nearby park. Assign groups of students to specific trees with instructions to measure their circumferences, draw a design of their leaves, report on the number of insects and birds found around each tree and finally complete a drawing of their trees. For the next four Fridays, walk your groups back to "their trees" to update their reports.

Students enjoy visiting their trees throughout the year. Each season they pick up blossoms, leaves or fruit to showcase on a science table.

Physical education To prepare your students for the year ahead, you might consider doing an exercise lesson daily when school begins. Model the exercises you wish to teach. If possible, have each student assigned to one spot for these group activities.

One school painted rows of large red dots with numbers on the blacktop. Each student was assigned a "spot" for the training. Begin slowly and work up to longer periods of exercise followed by a vigorous group activity such as soccer, kickball or dodgeball. Be aware of how many minutes of P.E. instruction your students should receive each week.

During the first month of school you'll learn much about your students—what their capabilities may be, whether you have some with problems and which ones you can depend upon for lessons and for classroom help. At the same time, they'll be judging you. Are you fair? Do you explain lessons and instructions well? Are lessons interesting and exciting? Have you set and maintained standards so everyone has a chance to learn? It's up to you to see that your early actions and interactions set the stage for a successful year for all of you.

9

Classroom Management

Recently I toured an automobile assembly plant. As I stood near the assembly line, a warning bell indicated a problem and the line was shut down. Immediately six people, men and women from several cultures, walked to a nearby table and sat down.

I could overhear them troubleshooting the problem. Each person participated and several suggestions were made. Within five minutes, they had solved the problem. They stood up, walked back to the line where the correction was made and the line restarted. This team of eager workers had collaborated with one goal in mind—to build the best pickup trucks possible.

For the last several years, "teamwork" has been a growing concept in American companies.

Why teams? In this country, we're no longer farmers plowing the fields alone. Instead, we're an information-gathering society. Many of our students will work on teams designing, writing and developing computer-software programs. Others will work in stores and factories and hospitals as part of a team.

To do this well, they need to learn academic subjects and also how to work successfully in groups. The atmosphere and style of your classroom can start developing teamwork.

Use the ideas in this chapter along with the resources in the Bibliography in the back of the book. Also, attend workshops on classroom management. Consider going on the Internet to join a teachers' group where you can share your management concerns with others.

What Is Classroom Management?

Effective classroom management is a method to empower students as they develop personal responsibility, character, orderliness and efficiency.

We must *teach* and model for students that *they* are responsible for their lives. Not the parents, the teacher, not society; *they alone* are making choices each day.

Students are not *born* responsible but they have the ability to learn responsibility. The first step is to introduce your management system immediately.

Who's running your room? There are three potential climates for your classroom.

- Teacher-empowered classroom

  The teacher makes all the rules and all the decisions. In this setting students learn that someone else is responsible for them.

- Student-empowered classroom

  Students take over, often leading to chaos. They decide if they will talk, learn or do nothing.

- Shared-empowered classroom

  This classroom operates as a democracy where both the teacher and students are empowered.

You'll find that the third style works best, both for maintaining a good learning atmosphere and for developing self-directed, responsible and caring students.

"Major myth is that children will suddenly have the 'aha' experience and become respectful and obedient as they grow older."

Dr. Ray Guarendi,
Psychologist

The importance of classroom management Teachers are concerned about their management systems and so are parents. In fact, for *years* the Gallup Poll has noted concern by parents about behavior in the classroom.

Keep in mind there's no "perfect" classroom-management system any more than there's one "perfect" solution for a specific problem. It's necessary that you continually develop a positive, cooperative climate in your classroom.

In a well-managed classroom, the teacher is an effective facilitator, and maximum student learning takes place. To do this you must:

- Be prepared.
- Be fair.
- Be consistent.

Why should you have a management system? First of all, for the safety of all students and to set limits on behavior and movement in the room. Also, to help students find acceptance, generate positive feelings and to encourage learning in the classroom.

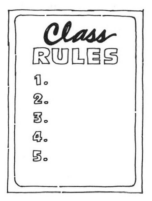

The key word here is *choice*. Students have a vested interest when they have some choice on how the classroom will function.

To meet these goals, you and your students must choose and establish effective classroom rules. They will be short, positive and easy to understand.

TEACHER TIP: Building bridges between teachers is vital, particularly for new teachers. Ask a staff member or a teacher in the district for assistance when needed, especially with issues like classroom management. Visit a coffeehouse with your colleague on a regular basis to discuss problems you're facing in the classroom.

Rules and Their Establishment

Laws and regulations are the basis of order in our country. In a similar manner the rules and procedures you use in your classroom are vital to the efficient running of a small schoolroom community. Depending upon your class, you'll need to spend

"Discipline requires a commitment to time and repetition."

Dr. Ray Guarendi,
Psychologist

A confident teacher is proactive when setting up rules and classroom structure.

Don't choose any rule you're not willing to enforce. If you fail to enforce even one of your rules, all the rest are suspect.

Frank Meder,
Veteran Teacher
Sacramento, CA

Your classroom rules should not conflict with your school's rules.

Sometimes more than five rules are too many.

Students who have a voice in establishing the rules are more likely to follow them.

Some rules, such as "no gum chewing in class," are not negotiable.

from two-to-four weeks at the beginning of the school year establishing your rules and routines.

Class rules help students know what's expected of them in the classroom, while school rules help them understand how to act outside the classroom.

For several weeks before school begins, think about the rules and routines you'll need in your classroom. The number and type will depend upon your school and grade level.

Even though you have rules in mind, you must collaborate with your students. At the beginning of the year, hold a class discussion on what and why rules are needed.

Point out to your students that there are two types of rules.

- *Broad* rules address general expectations and values regarding behavior and work habits.

- *Precise* rules set forth the specific procedures, classroom routines and standards for what will take place in the classroom, day in and day out.

Examples:

- Broad rule—Students are responsible for doing their best work on homework assignments.

- Precise rule—We will slowly walk single file to recess and lunch and the teacher will be at the end of the line.

```
┌─────────────────────────────────────────┐
│        Homework Checklist                │
│  Assignments for the week of_____      │
│  Math _____                           │
│  Language_____                        │
│  Rainbow Times_____                   │
│                                          │
│  Spelling test_____                   │
│                                          │
│  These assignments are missing:          │
│                                          │
│  Please Sign and Return_____          │
└─────────────────────────────────────────┘
```

After the rules have been agreed upon, ask small groups of students to each take one rule and as a group, explain *exactly* what it means. There should be no "cloudy" areas.

Use Signs to Visually Portray Positive Management

Posters and charts in the classroom colorfully showcase the management system. The signs are positive messages to students.

- Never settle for less than your best.
- If you believe it, you can achieve it.
- No one is a failure who keeps trying.

A basic value to promote in your students is respect, a commodity that seems to be diminishing in our society. For instance, handwaving while another student is talking is a common example of not being respectful to others. It's a good topic to discuss in your classroom. Guide students to discovering respectful alternatives such as having students use hand signs like those used by the deaf for "agree" and "disagree" instead of raising their hands. For "yes," students make a fist and move it slowly up and down. For "no," they make a fist and touch the thumb with the index and its neighbor finger.

Other ways for students to show they want to answer:

- Put empty paper cups on their desks.
- With elbows on table, rest chin on hands.
- Fold hands on desk tops.

Establish routines Routines and procedures should be taught the first month of school. Teaching takes place after a short reading or math lesson. Some suggestions follow:

- Model how you expect your students to walk in and out of the classroom each day. Ask a small group to role play.
- Demonstrate what will happen the first fifteen minutes of each day. You may have a different plan, but remember how helpful it is to have a consistent routine.
    - Will you have Show and Tell in primary grades?
    - Do you want to discuss one major current event in intermediate grades?
    - When will you take roll? Who will take the lunch and milk count? Can students collect papers?
- Discuss going to the bathroom and getting drinks.
- Talk about loud voices in the room. Is this respectful to others?

I know I can!

It's important to show respect for each other.

Hard work is the key to success.

When a new student enters the classroom, it's a good opportunity to reteach rules and routines.

Many students thrive on routines even if they don't have many at home.

- If students need help when the teacher is busy, what should they do? Solicit suggestions and steer toward solutions such as:

  - Ask someone else in the group.

  - Use a reference book.

  - Ask an aide or parent to help.

- Explain that students with free time may read a book, work at a learning center or work on the computer.

- Transitions—Your procedures for changing from one subject to the next must be addressed. Explain how this should be done. Be proactive. For example, have students put away journals and take out science books, pencils and graph paper before going out to recess.

Desk arrangements Some teachers prefer having desks in rows during the opening activities each morning. Later the students move their desks into groups. Other teachers prefer to keep desks in groups all the time. This will be your decision along with the class. But if you will be "movers," you must train your students to quickly and efficiently move desks from one arrangement to another.

When holding a Class Meeting, for example, it's important that students move desks into a circle. (See chapter on Class Meetings). Also, discuss desk arrangements when taking tests.

When I talk about pair and group work in this chapter, it simply refers to two or more students working together in the classroom. Some teachers call their desk arrangements "stations," "clusters" or "cooperative groups."

When rules and procedures are ignored When rules are broken or procedures are ignored, simply walk over to the offending student and in a normal voice, explain what was

Remember you have a lot more "clout" now when students are eager to go outside.

When and how often you'll have students move their desks during the day will depend upon the activities.

wrong and how to correct the problem. Speak in a voice so others can hear. Use these interruptions as "teaching moments" for all your students to observe.

Dr. Fred Jones in his book, *Positive Classroom Discipline*, discusses his ideas on how to deal with behavior problems in the classroom. He suggests that when a student disrupts the class, the teacher needs to turn around and directly face the youngster. At this time, say nothing but stare at the offender. Do this with a relaxed body which will exhibit self-confidence to the student.

Dr. Jones says, "A well-structured class means not only that the students know exactly what is expected of them but also that they have been trained and motivated to do it."

Extrinsic vs. Intrinsic Motivation

A goal in the classroom each day must be to help your students become lifelong, self-directed learners.

Extrinsic motivators become simply inducements to "do a job," while intrinsic motivation is the opposite. It means the child enjoys an activity simply for its own sake. This above all, puts the "joy" back in learning. When students operate in this mode, they forget time and sometimes keep doing the task longer than necessary.

An example is when students have and understand math skills but enjoy working on challenges, such as word problems. In fact, they're excited about a problem even when they must struggle to find answers.

Pair and Group Work

Alfie Kohn in his book, *Punished by Rewards*, discusses the importance of group work. Instead of having information handed to them, students become hunters and gatherers of information. Working in groups gives them an active role in learning.

Primary teachers often have their students work in pairs while intermediate teachers form groups using three or more children. Your room size and shape will determine how the desks will be placed. Allow plenty of space so you can "walk about" and yet see every student. This is called "having eyes in the back of your head."

TEACHER TIP: *Structure group activities so all members are successful. Each student must work with the others so success comes from the total group and not just one student.*

Use direct eye contact with a misbehaving student.

"We need to move away from the extrinsic rewards of stickers and candies and help students move toward becoming self-determined learners."

Alfie Kohn

"Our most important learning comes from our interaction with others."

Piaget

This is not the time for the "Lone Ranger" approach.

Research says uneven numbers in a group are better, but many classrooms function well with four working together.

Remember—two heads are better than one.

Sometimes there are three or four correct answers!

As teachers, we stress:
• Basic academic skills
• Gathering and processing information

As guides, we stress:
• Thinking skills
• Communication skills
• Social skills

Before launching group work, discuss with your class the importance of cooperating with other people. Give examples of where someone has assisted you, such as another teacher helping you carry a heavy box in from the car or a friend giving you a ride to school.

Have students discuss people who have helped them in some situation. Older brothers and sisters, for example, often will help younger students pump up their bike tires before they head for school.

The structure Group work can mean two, three or more students in a group. To begin, I'd suggest you start with three, placing a high, middle and low student in each group.

Primary teachers often use only two and may set up a buddy system. This sometimes enables one of the partners to be available to take work home when the other is absent.

Always allow time for each group's individuals to get to know each other. This might be a good time for a "two-minute, get-acquainted break."

Students may wish to name their group, make rules and select jobs such as the recorder, a resource person and a supply person.

The first lesson should be simple. Let's use the example of working together on a map labeling rivers in Alaska.

Remind students before they begin that you're looking for both academic and social skills in this lesson. This means they place the rivers' names on the map and describe how their group decided to gather the information. Did everyone take part in all of it, or were individual students responsible for different parts of the tasks? Comparing the approaches of various groups can lead to interesting discussions.

While the groups are working, walk around the room taking notes. Give feedback as you "walk about" or after the lesson is over.

Important skills While your class will ideally have a shared-empowered style of management, remember it will necessarily be task-oriented as well. Being task-oriented goes hand-in-hand with mastering necessary skills.

Our students must be taught the basic skills at each grade level. Point out that not all the work will be easy or fun but in a "group-sharing-caring" atmosphere each student can help the others.

Why social skills? Late one afternoon I asked my inner-city fourth graders, "What do you do after you leave this room each day?"

"I run home, open the door with this key," said one boy (pointing to a key hanging on a dirty string around his neck), "and I slam the door and lock it." Many other students nodded in agreement.

"Then," he continued, "I run around the house and be sure no one is hiding and then I turn on the television."

This frightened boy had to wait three nervous hours until his mother arrived home from work.

Many youngsters never go outside after school to play, especially if they live in a dangerous neighborhood. Since they can't interact with other children, they have few social skills.

Clearly, part of our daily activities must be aimed at helping students learn how to socialize and to become caring, respectful and mannerly human adults.

"If children are disrespectful and disobedient at age three, they will be even more so as they become teenagers."

Dr. Ray Guarendi,
Psychologist

Group work goes a long way toward this. It helps students deal with:

- Children from other cultures
- Youngsters with different languages
- Students from different economic families
- Boys and girls from a variety of family structures

Make your room a safe place where students can make mistakes and still be accepted.

A Boy Scout is:
• Trustworthy
• Loyal
• Helpful
• Friendly
• Courteous
• Kind
• Obedient
• Cheerful
• Thrifty
• Brave
• Clean and
• Reverent

Values The concept of values is closely related to social skills. In order for children to get along in this world, they must develop a set of values. I highly recommend *Teaching Your Children Values* by Linda and Richard Eyre. It gives a series of short lesson plans for teaching youngsters values such as honesty, courage, self-reliance and kindness. It's a most worthwhile book for parents and teachers. The Boy Scout Oath also stresses values.

To function in today's world, people have to interact more and more in group situations. School is the logical place to help students learn the necessary skills for working together.

The advantage of group work is that as students collaborate, they empower each other. They make choices which may or may not work, but they're free to make decisions about a task. As they explore the joy of learning, they also experience opportunities to share viewpoints. In addition, they learn and practice a variety of skills and learn the importance of values.

While teaching students to work together today, you're also preparing them to successfully live and work together as adults.

Class Meetings

While it's important that your students learn to read, do math and write, it's also essential that they learn how to solve problems and find solutions for themselves. This particular skill is a life-long legacy for students who sometimes see their world as a chaotic, frightening place over which they have little control.

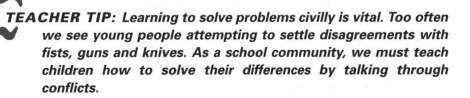

***TEACHER TIP:** Learning to solve problems civilly is vital. Too often we see young people attempting to settle disagreements with fists, guns and knives. As a school community, we must teach children how to solve their differences by talking through conflicts.*

One place to develop your students' problem-solving skills is during your daily Class Meeting. Surprisingly, surveys indicate fewer than 20 percent of all teachers conduct such meetings. Those who don't are overlooking a valuable, proactive management tool.

 CAUTION: Don't initiate Class Meetings until you're well prepared. Perhaps the school counselor could come to your room and conduct several for you to observe. You might also arrange to visit a classroom which holds them in your district. To purchase a video showing an actual Class Meeting, call 800-262-4387.

Many of the problems you'll deal with relate to situations which arise between students in your classroom or on the playground. Most of these disagreements can be solved at a Class Meeting. Other times, more personal problems (and sometimes home problems) will arise. When they do, be sure you're aware of resources not only within your school staff but also in the community.

What Is a Class Meeting?

It's an organized, orderly discussion time where teacher and students collaborate to create a positive classroom environment. Discussion topics will include behavior issues as well as activities and curriculum planning.

Primary classroom A primary teacher must deal with three common problems:

- Tattling
- Arguments about not taking turns
- Fighting over equipment such as jump ropes and balls

As a primary teacher you'll quickly discover that much of your day can be nibbled away by students who continually tattle on others. In fact, some years can be plagued with an overabundance of "tattlers."

Intermediate classroom In the intermediate grades "tattling" progresses to:

- Sharing secrets
- Love/hate notes being passed around
- Outright hostility such as pushing and shoving or worse

To cope with these ongoing issues and still have time to teach, plan to conduct a Class Meeting daily.

Prepare your class by explaining that you're not an umpire or referee. Students will have to bring up their issues at the Class

Suggested lengths of time for Class Meetings:
- Kindergarten—20 minutes
- Primary—25 minutes
- Intermediate—30 minutes

Meeting. Some problems to address in Class Meetings are squabbling, fighting and name-calling. Discuss with your students the need to put problems on the "agenda." You'll need to be firm about this.

Emphasize, however, that you'll always accept "reporting" which means telling when a student is ill, injured or has been threatened by others.

Set a timer to go off 5-7 minutes before the end of the Class Meeting. This will alert you to conclude your current discussion and not begin another.

The agenda The "agenda" can be kept in a binder with a pencil attached by a string for instant use. Place the binder near an exit with easy access for all students. Tell them they can write in the agenda only at certain times such as:

- On the way out to recess or lunch
- As they leave to go home at the end of the day

On an overhead projector or the chalkboard, illustrate how students are to write on the agenda.

- List the date.
- List the complaining student's name in the name column.
- Name the person the student wishes to discuss.
- Briefly state the problem.

NOTE: Use a prearranged signal to alert your students to prepare for the Class Meeting.

Before your first meeting, decide upon the days and time to hold them if you can't do it daily. Plan also how you'll arrange the room for the meeting. Set a natural ending time by scheduling meetings before lunch, before afternoon recess or the end of the day.

Room arrangement The best arrangement is often for the students to be assigned seats in a circle.

- All students can see each other.
- Each student has a sense of equality.
- Using chairs adds more structure to the meeting.
- Assigning seats minimizes disruptions.

Before conducting the first meeting, you and your students should discuss how the meeting will be run.

The Teacher-as-Facilitator

The Teacher-as-Facilitator meeting is carried out with the teacher being present but doing little of the talking. He or she indicates which group will be first to push desks to the side of the room and take their chairs into the circle. The meeting begins after all students and chairs have been moved.

Conduct the meeting Explain that you'll *always* open by hearing compliments. Then model a compliment such as, "Taylor, I like the way you took the time to help Angelo find his library book today." Or, "Carly, I appreciate your helping the kindergarten teacher calm down little Luis this morning."

For the most part, the meeting flows along with the students' own "give and take," yet it's based on the structure which was taught before the first meeting. This structure is built upon respect between teacher and students and is reinforced by certain ground rules:

- Listen to others.
- Take turns.
- Make recommendations.

Remind students that meetings are held so all can work together to solve problems and help each other.

Next move on to issues needing attention.

Open the discussion portion of the meeting by using the agenda binder which should have a running diary of issues entered by students. For example, you might say, "Nicole, you wrote in the agenda three days ago that Tony pulled your hair. Has this been settled or should we consider it today?"

If the problem has been solved, compliment the students who were involved. If not, Tony should be asked to explain his action.

➡ NOTE: To cut down on vocal interruptions, introduce the class to "hand signals." During a discussion, students who agree can give a "yes" sign by moving the hand (at the wrist) up and down quietly. To disagree, students move their hand from side to side like an umpire's "safe" signal.

Tony says he pulled Nicole's hair because she cut in line. Some hands go up and down in agreement, but most move side to side. Next solicit suggestions as to what should be done and allow several minutes of discussion as you condense and write down ideas.

These discussions will help students understand "logical consequences" and show them how to distinguish between consequences and punishment. After discussion, you should read the students' suggestions for remedying problems. The students can determine which ones are *logical* (suitable) and which ones are not.

For example, describe Sarah walking through puddles after a rainstorm on the way home. Ask, "What do you suppose might happen?"

Students will often reply, "Sarah could get wet and could catch a cold." Point out that this is a natural consequence.

A logical consequence might be that her mother keeps Sarah in the house while she is running a fever. Spanking her would not be logical. Give several more examples until you're sure the children understand the concept.

To lead students to greater insight into behavior and misbehavior, present questions such as:

- What do you think about this?
- What do you think we should do?
- Why do you suppose she did that?
- How could we help Michael feel better today?

During the first few meetings present plenty of examples. Later describe situations for the students to interpret for practice.

➡ NOTE: The teacher has the right to stop the meeting at any time to ask a question.

The 4 R's for logical consequences are:
• Related to the problem
• Reasonable
• Respectful
• Responsible

Most of your Class Meetings will deal with small annoyances such as name calling, playing in the bathroom or spitting. For more serious problems, look at the chapter on Classroom Management.

Your students can request that a child from another room come to the Class Meeting if the youngster is involved in an issue. This requires a higher level of experience with Class Meetings and should not be done until after you and your class know the routine and can handle it proficiently.

When the bell signals the end of the meeting, bring it to a close. Some students may not have had an opportunity to air their concerns. Simply say, "We'll try to cover this at the next meeting."

Responsibility of the teacher While you want your students to take as much responsibility as they can for their Class Meetings, you still have the ultimate responsibility for those meetings. You must oversee them while the students are learning, but how well you guide them will determine their understanding and ability to later conduct them mostly by themselves.

Take notes as suggestions are made for misbehavior consequences. Ask students to assist in deciding what should be done to solve each issue. Sometimes only an apology is needed, but for more serious misbehaviors, discussions may include a consequence.

As each suggestion is given, make notes on the agenda, and then ask for comments. Some proposals made in our examples include:

- Tony should apologize to Nicole.
- He should apologize and be the last in line this week.
- He should apologize and go to the end of the line after the morning recess.

Your body language should clearly tell your students that you're pleased when they behave, compliment each other and show good manners. On the other hand, when a student continues to get into trouble, your demeanor should impart your sense of disappointment and concern that a member of your class would behave in such a manner.

Remind students that meetings are held so everyone can work together to solve problems and help each other. After a solution is agreed upon, each student then has an opportunity to give his or her reaction to the consequences and tips for future improvement.

Solving small problems now should prevent more serious problems in the future.

Students often suggest carefully considered options.

It's also very important to teach your students the four main reasons for misbehavior:

- To get attention
- To demonstrate being powerful
- To get revenge
- To claim they can't do anything, which in turn, reinforces their need for attention

When you and your students are aware of these causes for misbehavior, you can address them during the Class Meeting. They could influence the choice of consequences. For example, a student who wants attention might act silly while playing baseball. Or, during math might yell out, "I can't do this math."

When problems arise regarding student behavior or even with the Class Meeting itself, it's important that your students be encouraged to participate in solutions.

- Ask students' opinions, yet keep them on the topic.
- Avoid being any type of police magistrate.

At class meetings, model for your students how to get along with classmates from other cultures.

- If a humiliating statement is made such as, "He's so stupid," ask, "How many people would like to be called 'stupid'?"
- After initial meetings, student input will increase.

Don't expect to be perfect. You'll make mistakes because solving social problems is not easy.

Besides learning problem-solving techniques, your class will also develop language skills, leadership potential and the ability to refine thoughts and ideas.

Although setting up Class Meetings takes time, and the proceedings may seem artificial and stilted at first, you'll find the benefits are very real. Older students will be able to run a Class Meeting with very little guidance from you. All will learn to be more considerate in their relations with others. They will also become more realistic about assessing the behavior of their peers and about their expectations of results if others misbehave.

Back-to-School Night—Open House

Whether you're teaching six grades in a two-room log schoolhouse or one of six first grades at a large urban school, you need parent support. One way schools can gain parent backing is to hold a Back-to-School Night during the first month of school.

In this chapter you'll discover how to plan a successful Back-to-School Night as well as a spring Open House to show what your students have been doing all year. Part of this chapter will also be devoted to showing kindergarten teachers how to hold a Parent-Orientation Meeting prior to the opening of school.

TEACHER TIP: *More and more schools nationwide are urging parents to come to meetings, help with their children's homework and take an active part in their youngsters' schooling. A helpful book for parents of children aged three to twelve is my* **Parent Power—A Guide to Your Child's Success.**

Back-to-School-Night Invitations

Some school districts send prepared invitations. Others send out a weekly Parent Newsletter, including information about Back-to-School Night.

Having the students design and write their own invitations to their parents is a wonderful way for youngsters to take part in this activity. Consider doing this with your class and include the following information:

- Name of the school and address
- Date of the Back-to-School Night
- Time
- Room number
- Teacher's name

Have students design an invitation.
- Young students can decorate preprinted invitations.
- Have a written lesson for older students.

🍎 **TEACHER TIP:** *Many children today come from split homes and frequently only one parent comes to school, since the other parent lives elsewhere. In such situations, see if your student wants a separate invitation for each parent. Also, suggest the child bring an inexpensive camera to Back-to-School Night and take pictures for the missing parent to enjoy.*

Classroom Preparation

Fresh flowers are a welcoming touch.

For many parents' first glimpse of their children's new teacher and classroom, you want to give the best possible impression of your teaching abilities.

Room arrangement The following checklist for your room preparation may be photocopied and used as an example:

- A sign outside your classroom stating the room number and showing a colorfully printed "Welcome"

- Your name and room number written on the chalkboard
- Fresh flowers which students can bring
- Sign-in sheet for parents
- Sign-up sheets for parent conferences, guest speakers and helpers
- Adult chairs for those who might have problems sitting at small desks
- Daily schedule written on the chalkboard
- Bright bulletin boards showing special study information
- Display of classroom textbooks
- Names on all desks
- Clean desks both inside and out

Examples of student work Parents are anxious to see their children's work.

- Have folders on each desk with samples of what the students have done.
- Samples of students' work on a bulletin board allow parents to compare their child's efforts with those of classmates.
- Post snapshots you've taken to show a typical day.

Photos on Bulletin Board:
- Classroom tutors
- Students working on a class project
- Parents helping in the room
- A P.E. activity

Teacher Preparation

Personal Dressing for success is important because it transfers over into your attitude, "I'm an outstanding teacher and I'm proud to be in the profession."

Women should wear a nice outfit and men should wear a suit or sweater, dress shirt and tie and well-polished shoes.

To put your best foot forward, be sure your shoes are shined!

Your presentation Again, as on the first day of school, you need to be overprepared. Make notes to be sure all points are covered, including yourself, your policies and procedures and your goals.

- Give a brief personal background including your own schooling and your philosophy of education.
- Present your goals for the year.

Briefly list and explain the school's and your *basic policies*, *procedures* and *plans* for the coming year.

- Daily schedule
- Group placement and program for split classes
- Homework—how often and when to return it with a parent's signature. Makeup policy if a child is sick
- Grading
- Your five classroom rules and management system
- Field trips and special programs
- Parties and fund raisers
- Ways to meet individual needs such as remedial help for low achievers and programs available for gifted students
- Where students will turn in completed assignments and where they are to pick up corrected work
- How parents can help their children regarding homework routines, spelling practice and signing off on assignments

🍎 *TEACHER TIP: Remember the most important gift you can give parents is the feeling that their child matters to you. Parents send their children to you each day to help them learn to become worthwhile citizens. Let your caring show.*

After your brief presentation

- Invite questions.
- Conclude the meeting and invite parents to stay.
- As you circulate, give a warm smile, firm handshake and a positive word about each child.
- If some parents monopolize your time, say, "I would be happy to meet with you for an appointment another time."
- If your P.T.A. has planned a coffee hour after the meeting, encourage your parents to attend.
- After the parents all leave, join your faculty for a time of socializing at a nearby restaurant.

> **TEACHER TIP:** *Although teaching itself is an "alone" job, you should include time for celebrations after meetings and at faculty parties for a job well done. You'll gain new ideas, socialize with other teachers and find you are not alone.*

Kindergarten-Orientation Meeting

If you are a kindergarten teacher, arrange an orientation for all new kindergartners in your class the week before school begins, if at all possible. The experience will be helpful for the children and reassuring to the parents.

Room arrangement Your room should be spotlessly clean, with bright bulletin boards and five-year-old-sized tables and chairs. If possible, provide adult chairs as well.

- Write your class schedule on the chalkboard.
- Provide a sign-up sheet for bus riders.
- Post the current breakfast or lunch menu on the board, if appropriate.

Teacher presentation Both men and women need to dress professionally. For example, men wear slacks and a sport coat and women a nice dress. Sit on a kindergarten-sized chair to talk

You and the parents are a team.

Kindergarten invitations should list: Who? What? Where? When? and Why?

with the parents and your new kindergartners. Your presentation should not be more than fifteen minutes. Allow time for questions afterward. Include the following topics:

- Regular attendance is important.
- Parents must send absence excuses or requests for early dismissal.
- Announce the earliest time students may arrive, when a playground teacher will be on duty.
- Tell which days children will participate in Show and Tell.
- Children shouldn't bring expensive toys for Show and Tell.
- Give dates for parent conferences.
- Children must be able to recite their full names, addresses and telephone numbers.
- It's vital that children learn to take care of their personal belongings such as coats, hats and lunch pails.
- Children should wear suitable, washable clothes for sitting on the floor, painting and playing in the schoolyard.

A child must wear safe sturdy shoes, *not*:
- Slippery, plastic sandals
- Shoes without toes

- Label everything brought to school.
- Stress the importance of walking directly to school and not playing along the way.
- Discuss good safety habits of not talking to or riding with strangers.
- It's important that a child knows whether to go to a baby sitter, relative or home after school.
- Classroom volunteers are needed daily.
- Explain that each child will be given a diagnostic test after school begins to determine learning strengths and weak areas.

- Ask parents to send a small snack each day for their children.
- Parents must sign a bus sheet if their children will ride the bus.

For safety's sake and for children speaking limited English, it's especially important that students know their names, addresses and telephone numbers. They also must also know where to get off the bus.

✔ SUGGESTION: Provide a sign-up sheet for parent volunteers in your classroom. Kindergarten teachers often have the luxury of more volunteers than any other grade level. Use them!

Cookie time After your meeting, invite parents to stay and visit over cookies and punch or coffee. Greet the children and tell them how much you're looking forward to having them in your classroom. Show your pleasure at having so many parents attend; take the time to spend a short time with each one.

Open House

Back-to-School Night is when you *tell* parents and the community what you're going to do during the school year. Open House is when you *show* them what you've done.

It's our way of saying, "Look at all the good things going on." We're proud of what your children are doing and what we, as teachers, are doing. Come and visit us."

At many schools, parents are invited to visit classrooms, have lunch with their children in the cafeteria and attend an Open House either one afternoon or evening. Some schools include a Science Fair as a way of showing outstanding science projects constructed by students at all grade levels.

In this section you'll find ideas for putting on a successful Open House as well as a Science Fair.

Get ideas for your Open House If you're a student teacher, try to attend an Open House sometime before you hold your first one and do the following:

- Make notes on outstanding displays.

- Bring your camera along and take pictures.

- Visit the faculty room and make notes on titles of teachers' magazines to which you can subscribe for ideas for your first Open House.

- Ask other teachers for ideas which have proved successful at your grade level. Always be on the lookout for creative projects.

Prepare in advance Start thinking "Open House" in September so you'll have everything you need without rushing to get projects done at the last minute. Don't make it an overwhelming project, however. Begin early, stay calm and do your best while keeping it as simple as possible.

Suggestions from veteran teachers include:

- Save sample reading, language and math papers beginning in September.
- Post at least three samples of work for each student.
- Insist that all posted work must be neat, clean and well-done.
- Use Open House as a time to continue your year-long instruction in, "Be responsible and do your best work."
- Have students create a mural based on a field trip or social studies unit.
- String a wire across the room and hang up art projects with brightly colored clothespins.

Preparations for the week before Open House

- Designate one student to prepare a guest book.
- Have another student who will sit next to the book and be sure everyone signs it.
- Have another student assigned to prepare a tally of the number of parents and students who attend.
- Be sure all names are on students' desks.
- Even if the school sends out a "blanket invitation" to parents, have your students write personal letters to their parents.

Have a clothesline art show.

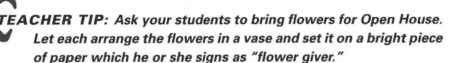

TEACHER TIP: *Ask your students to bring flowers for Open House. Let each arrange the flowers in a vase and set it on a bright piece of paper which he or she signs as "flower giver."*

Open-House night Allow yourself plenty of prep time. With good planning, you should have finished all displays, bulletin boards and desk cleaning the day before Open House.

Leave school as soon as possible on Open-House day to relax at home. Dress for success, arrive back at school a few minutes early and be prepared to have a wonderful time.

When you arrive, open some windows for fresh air. Be sure the custodian emptied all waste baskets and that desks and chairs are in order. As parents and students arrive, be warm and friendly. While you show them where to find their children's papers, have something positive to say about each child. Don't let any parents monopolize your time, and be sure to greet each person promptly.

> **TEACHER TIP:** *Prior to the Open House, review parents' names so you can greet them individually. Remember, some of your students and parents may have different last names. Be cautious about saying, "I've been looking forward to meeting Marcia's father." He may be Marcia's mother's boyfriend or second husband.*

Time to go:
- Set your timer to ring.
- Dim the lights.
- Erase the boards.
- Turn off the computers.

After the Open House Be friendly but firm when the time for Open House has ended. Begin to turn off lights, shut down the computer and put display books away.

Afterward meet some of your fellow teachers for a time of relaxation, rehashing and rejoicing that you not only survived Open House but had a great time!

Science Fair

One way to extend the scope of the Open House is to encourage parents to work with their children on a science exhibit which will be displayed either for the entire school or for your room. At least a month before the Science Fair, send home a sheet which includes the following information:

Guidelines for science projects

- There's a limit of one exhibit per child.
- Parents may help, but students should do most of the work.
- Suggestions for primary students:
    - Do a model from a kit such as the heart or lungs.
    - Make an exhibit of an animal habitat.
    - Plant seeds.
    - Do a study of various flowers or grasses.
- Primary students should title their exhibits and write a paragraph about their findings.
- Intermediate students should write a one-page summary and give the following information:
    - State the problem—what you want to show or find out.
    - State how you'll solve your problem or learn about it.
    - Finally, present your conclusion—what you learned when you did the study.

General guidelines for exhibits

- Use tagboard or cardboard with the title printed clearly at the top.
- Use three sheets of tagboard joined together with masking tape for large displays so the chart can stand and be seen from a distance.
- If batteries, extension cords or special lighting are needed, the student should supply these items.
- Give the judging date and tell where students should take their exhibits.
- Provide names of those on the judging committee.
- Let students know what awards will be given.
- Alert students when exhibits should go home after Open House.

Example of a successful Science-Fair project One teacher called her local Park District in October for help on a science unit about wood. The District Ranger visited the classroom to talk about the importance of trees in the community. Afterward the teacher divided the students into groups of four and had each group plant one tree seed, provided by the ranger, in a can filled with rich soil.

During the school year, students took turns watering their trees, charting their growth and taking the saplings home during vacations. By April the trees were more than two feet tall and the class entered them in the Science Fair.

♣ HINT: Have the exhibits completed and judged at least one week before your Open House. This will reduce last-minute hassles.

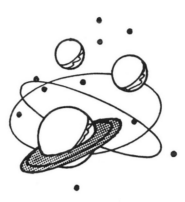

Other year-long projects:
• Study a local fish.
• Research planets.
• Grow microbes.

Look for simple ideas which can work into classroom projects for an entire year, giving students an opportunity to learn and to give something back to their community at the same time.

Report Cards and Parent Conferences

"**W**hat'd ya get?" is the BIG question four times each year in classrooms across the country as students compare their grades. For teachers, the method of arriving at "the grade" is frequently a long, difficult, paper-filled process. You'll find that by keeping good records week-by-week you'll have a head start when report-card time rolls around.

The Step-by-Step Reporting Procedure

Keep parents informed This is the "watchword" for teachers to heed. Parents want to know how their child is doing. They don't want their lives interrupted by a negative phone call from a teacher relating something they've never heard about before.

♣ HINT: To save yourself many hours of future distress, always keep parents informed about a child's behavior problems, academic deficiencies or failure to appear at school. The extra effort

Over the years, I discovered negative notices seldom make it home. I've found the U.S. Post Office is much more dependable than a student, and it's worth the price of a stamp to know messages reach parents.

you put forth early will save you later from being accused of "never letting us know until the last minute."

Deficiency notices Many school districts require that several weeks before report cards go out, teachers send home deficiency notices for all students doing below-grade-level work in specific subject areas or having behavior problems.

Sometimes notices come with carbon-sensitive pages attached. The parent signs one copy which the student returns to the teacher by a specific date. The bottom copy is retained by the parent and one copy is placed by the teacher in the permanent record folder of the student.

Class register Some schools use the traditional class registers to indicate absent and tardy students. Others have a person in the office who tracks attendance on a computer. Check with your school secretary to find out how you're expected to keep attendance.

NOTE: Rating grades will depend upon your school district. Many no longer give letter grades but mark "S" for satisfactory, "I" for improvement needed and "U" for unsatisfactory. Other districts ask teachers to provide conventional grades.

Portfolios Many teachers keep ongoing written examples showing what each child can do. This is a collaborative team process between teacher and student. Together they explore and talk about the progress of the child. During the year, let the parents know you're keeping schoolwork for the portfolio and at conferences, go over the portfolio together.

The grading system in the primary and intermediate grades You'll soon discover that there is often a discrepancy between grades given by primary teachers and intermediate teachers.

Some primary teachers are accused by intermediate teachers of being too soft on grading, trying to please parents and not being realistic about a student's academic ability.

Intermediate teachers complain that when a student comes to them in fourth, fifth or sixth grade, he or she may not be doing the "A"-level work that had been reported and, for the first time, parents are faced with a "C" grade, or lower. In turn, parents blame intermediate teachers who must justify why a lower grade is warranted now.

The "C" grade Because of "grade creep," a "C" grade is often looked upon as being a negative grade much like a "D." We need to remind parents that "C" is average, and average is normal, not bad.

The children may *all* be "above average" in the fictional town of Lake Wobegon, but not many other places.

Keep good records In order to back up grades, and especially in the case of retention, you *must* keep accurate records which include:

- Weekly spelling test grades
- Oral and comprehension reading scores
- Reading unit test grades
- Math unit test grades
- A graded sample from language papers
- Social studies and science unit grades
- Oral reports
- Handwriting samples with scores
- Citizenship grades
- A weekly grade from each subject area

🍎 **TEACHER TIP:** *Begin the first week of school to keep a folder on each student and drop in samples of tests, daily work, spelling tests and even art work. These folders will serve as a "reminder" to you as you begin to consult your grade book to do report cards. You can also use these folders at conferences as a visible way of illustrating the grades given.*

Prepare your students for "their" report cards

Beginning the first month of school, set aside a lesson time in social studies to teach about report cards and each student's responsibility for grades.

SIX WEEKS REPORTING PERIODS

SUBJECT	1ST	2ND	3RD	4TH	5TH	6TH	AVG
READING	/	/	/	/	/	/	
LANGUAGE							
WRITING							
SPELLING							
MATH							
SCIENCE							
SOC. STUDIES							
HEALTH							
P.E.							
FINE ARTS MUSIC/ART	/	/	/	/	/	/	
CONDUCT							

🍎 **TEACHER TIP:** *Constantly remind your students throughout the year that they're choosing how they will act. Too many students will say, for example, "He made me write on the principal's car," or "She made me talk in the assembly!" Students need to know that no one makes them do anything. They alone are choosing every moment what they'll do next.*

Students *choose* to study or not to study.

Fully 70 percent of children in foster-home care have one or both parents on drugs. How to choose what is good and productive is an important lesson to teach early in our schools.

Students will come to you thinking *you give them* the grades. You must let them know up front that *they earn every grade they receive.* At the same time, constantly hold discussions on the importance of learning and why students come to school each day.

Here are some suggestions:

- Tell the class when report cards will come out.
- Give each child a blank report card, or reproduce one for use on the overhead.
- Point out the section titled "Work Habits" and explain what this means.
- Have students look at "Social Skills" and choral read: "Respects rights/property of others, Demonstrates self-control, Solves problems appropriately and Observes class/school rules." Discuss each skill.
- Ask your students questions such as: What does it mean to be reading *"Below* grade level"? *"Above* grade level"? How would it feel to be reading *"below level"* or *"above level"*?
- What could *you* do to improve *your* reading grade?
- Spend time on "Record of Attendance." Discuss the importance of coming to school in order to learn and get smarter.
- Point out the line which reads, "Assignment for Next Year" and discuss the importance of moving up the ladder of learning.
- Talk about the comments written on the report card.
- Tell students a copy of their report cards will go into their permanent folders in the office.
- Define an "A" grade, "B," "C," "D" and "F."

Work on report cards Plan ahead for filling out report cards. If you don't, the time will arrive and you'll be rushed to do a task which requires far more time than you expect. Begin to assemble all student folders, your attendance materials and grade book at least a week before grades are to go home.

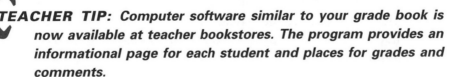

TEACHER TIP: Computer software similar to your grade book is now available at teacher bookstores. The program provides an informational page for each student and places for grades and comments.

Report card comments These need not be long, but they should be specific. Example: If a student is doing average work, you need only write, "Making average progress. Reading on grade level and has accomplished five out of 10 levels in math."

Most students see a report card for the first time when they carry it home.

Keep in mind that in many schools, letter grades are either not given or are given only at particular levels.

For an above-average student you could say, "Making excellent progress. Randy is an outstanding oral reader."

If a student is working below average, you might say, "Making below-average progress. Has accomplished 3 out of 8 levels in reading and 4 out of 10 levels in math."

Some students will come into your room working below grade level and continue to accomplish little. Now is the time to reach out for help within your school district. This might be a "Caring Committee" made up of the principal, counselor, nurse and resource teacher. As quickly as possible, seek help for the student.

Retention This is an ongoing problem for both new and veteran teachers each year as they do report cards and hold parent conferences. Rightly so.

Some children who are not prepared for kindergarten seem to do much better when they don't enter school until the following year. In fact, some schools' kindergartners are given a brief test before school begins. If a student isn't ready for school, the parents are provided with suggestions for working with their child for a year before the youngster begins kindergarten.

NOTE: "Social promotion" is being questioned throughout the country. It's imperative that you have your principal define district policy in this matter. However, if retention is being considered, talk with the parents as early as possible. Further discussion will be found in Chapter 18.

When speaking to a parent about a child's deficiencies, always remember to begin by discussing the child's strengths, because every child has some.

Look in the student's folder to see if mention is made of visual or hearing problems. These need to be checked out.

If you're not sure how well a student will function the following year, you might consider using a contract with the parent and child. Note subjects needing improvement and comments to help a tutor or summer-school teacher. When school begins, retest the child. Meet with the parent, child and counselor and go over the summer's progress before making a decision on retention.

TEACHER TIP: *Never let your own personal likes or dislikes of a particular student influence the grades you record. Let the folder of samples, plus your grade book, tell the story. You must be fair to each child in your classroom.*

Citizenship grades During the school year use the following phrases in your classroom:

- You choose
- You're choosing

Permanent files After you complete all report cards, you'll need to enter the academic grades, days present and absent and citizenship grades on the students' permanent files in the office.

See if you also need to enter reading, math and language levels and unit-test grades on special forms in each permanent record. Some principals require this at each report card or parent-conference period, while others permit teachers to do this paperwork at the end of the year.

When children make choices, they're also grading themselves.

TEACHER TIP: *With so many families on the move, it's best to keep the permanent files up-to-date. This way when a student moves, you don't have to spend the extra time updating the file before it's sent to the next school.*

Parent Conferences

A Parent Conference is a personal meeting between you and the parents or guardians of one of your students. It provides a time when additional information about the child can be brought out, samples of work examined jointly and questions answered.

One intermediate teacher devised a particularly clever memo to tell parents about their child's strengths and weaknesses. As she talks to parents, she jots down key phrases on her "Kid Scoop" form. She makes a carbon copy to keep and gives the form itself to the parents.

TEACHER TIP: *If you're a student teacher, request that prior to your graduation, your master teacher invites you to sit in and observe several Parent Conferences. As soon as possible after the meeting, jot down notes on procedure, room arrangement and bookkeeping methods. The information gained will be invaluable to you when you conduct your own Parent Conferences, and you'll feel much more confident after observing a veteran teacher in action.*

Prior-to-the-conference strategies You'll be nervous when it's time to conduct your first conference, but keep in mind that the parents may be, too. Surveys indicate that many parents hate to come to school. They're sure the teacher will tell them only *bad* things about their child, show them a report card filled with "D" grades and even, perhaps, suggest the child be retained.

NOTE: Starting several weeks before your conferences, remind parents in each weekly newsletter you're looking forward to meeting them. You might say, "By working together, we can ensure a wonderful and constructive year for your child." This will help to take away some of the parents' apprehension. Also, remind them to sign and return the conference letter you send home so you can confirm their names on your conference schedule.

Always start with a positive statement about each child and be sure to have one ready for all your students.

Conference preparations There are a number of things you'll need to do before Parent Conferences:

- Complete all report cards.
- File all sample work and tests in students' conference folders.
- Fill out a Parent-Conference schedule for yourself and the office.
- Make changes on your list as notices are returned.
- Review notes on each child, parents' names and any ongoing behavior problems noted during the year.
- Have a sample of each textbook available.
- File all information to share with a child's parents into one folder with the child's name, day and date of conference on the front.
- Arrange folders for each day according to your Parent-Conference schedule.
- Have students *really clean* their desks.

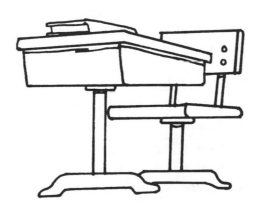

- Check to see if your district will give you a work day prior to the conference.

 TEACHER TIP: *If you are given a "work day" prior to the first conference, use the day only for your preparation. Don't schedule any conferences on that day so you'll have time to get ready. You'll be better prepared, more relaxed and more confident to begin.*

♣ HINT: If possible, use a table for your Parent Conferences. Many parents are more comfortable talking to a teacher over a table rather than a big, official-looking desk.

A small bouquet of cheerful flowers lends a welcoming air.

Room arrangement Use a checklist as you prepare your classroom for Parent Conferences:

- Have a table available for conferences.
- Have three or four adult-sized chairs placed around the table.
- If adult chairs are not available, be sure you sit on a student chair yourself.
- Have paper, pencils and "Kid Scoops" available.
- Have the Parent-Conference schedule in front of you on the table. Either sit at the table facing the classroom clock or have one nearby.
- If there are no benches outside your room, place two chairs outside the door for parents who arrive early and must wait.
- If parents must wait outdoors, arrange for them to wait in the office if the weather is bad. No other person should be in your room during a conference unless you're conferencing at night.
- Ask your principal what your district recommends regarding students attending Parent Conferences.
- Ask your principal beforehand for suggestions if parents bring younger children along. Is it possible to have them play outside? Wait in the office? His or her recommendations?

Guidelines for a successful conference:

- Greet parents with a firm handshake and use their names as you invite them inside.
- Always begin on a positive note and say, "I've enjoyed having Jeremy or Janie in my classroom this year."
- Don't do all the talking. Leave plenty of time for parents to speak and ask questions.
- If parents disagree with your evaluation or challenge you, let them have their say. At the end say, "I understand what you're saying. Let's see if we can work this out together."
- If you aren't sure what they mean, paraphrase the statement and say, "Is this what you're saying?"
- Don't simply label a student "lazy" or "unmotivated." Rather, give an illustration such as, "Janie sat for 20 minutes yesterday looking out the window and didn't do her spelling." Let your "word pictures" do the talking.
- Serve as a resource person to the parents of the child if needed. Example: If the child is showing emotional problems, say, "I'll be happy to refer Janie to our school counselor for testing."

Keep on the subject. If the discussion turns to problems apart from the student, bring the conversation back to that child.

- If you don't have a school counselor, have available a list of nearby counseling services with names, addresses and telephone numbers which the parents can jot down.
- If a student is having continual problems with homework and the parents ask for help, have a list of resources such as:
  - A local homework hot line telephone number
  - A list of available tutors
  - A list of after-school programs
  - Names of schools for evening student help
  - Information on television channels or Internet homework hot lines
- Provide ideas for ways parents can help a child at home. My book, *Parent Power—A Guide to Your Child's Success*, offers detailed help in all subject areas.
- Ask parents for feedback, as well. Ask what works for them when helping their child at home in reading. In math. In changing behavior problems. Share your resources for the good of the student.
- Emphasize to parents that you genuinely care about their child.
- Finally, let them know they can call for another appointment.

> If possible, obtain copies of referral suggestions so the parents can take a personal copy home.

> Don't rush on conference days. Allow time to eat lunch and relax. Have all materials ready at your desk/table.

A few additional suggestions for the conference day can be helpful.

- In your Monday Memo prior to conferences, explain that seating will be provided outside your door if parents arrive early. Ask them not to knock and that you'll meet them at the door on time for their appointment.

- Dress for success.
- Have all your folders near you in order of appointment times.
- Be well prepared with everything inside the folders.
- Place the report card inside the folder.
- Keep your copy of the report card out to file later into the permanent-record folder.
- Have paper and pencil handy for note taking.
- Have your register, grade book and anecdotal notes in order as references if requested.
- Be aware of each reading level and math level for each student.
- Schedule one or two short breaks to relax during your conferences.

Parent Conferences can be helpful for both you and your students, especially those who are having problems of any kind. Be sure to make their parents aware of these problems early. Then seek input and cooperation from all, including the student, in working to turn around the situation.

Have a glass of water handy, as you'll be talking a great deal. Also, keep mouthwash or breath mints nearby.

Field Trips/Fund Raisers/Classroom Speakers

Field trips serve as a vehicle for getting students out into their community. They provide variety, first-hand information and a change of pace from the "dailyness" of the classroom. Use them.

Planning

If possible, even before school starts, plan the majority of your field trips. As you go through the district's curriculum guides, make notes on what your students should learn during the year and have some of that learning occur outside the classroom. If funds are limited, see the following section on "Fund Raisers."

Ask your school secretary for your district's field-trip binder. It should include:

- Field trips available
- Grade-level designations
- Listing of days, hours and length of visit
- Maximum number of students accepted

Check with your school secretary for the paperwork needed to take your class on local field trips. Do this early—as often, few buses are available.

If possible, plan one out-of-town field trip on a bus each year.

- Number of parents required to accompany class
- Contact person and telephone number
- Any fees

The secretary should be able to provide you with the forms to be completed and give you the telephone number of the field-trip office so you can check on available dates for trips and buses.

TEACHER TIP: *Some field trips are much more popular than others, so place your request as early as possible to get the date you'd like. Always have a backup trip in mind, in case your first choice is already taken.*

At some schools certain field trips are traditional for particular grades.

Plan your field trip as a "grand finale" to a unit you've been studying. The following example ties science to art and language, then goes "on the road."

Go fish Each November, one primary teacher presents a science unit on fish. He uses several ideas which help motivate students to become involved.

- Hang mobiles of fish from the ceiling.
- Design a bulletin board titled "Going Fishing," complete with fishing net and student-designed fish, seashells and sea stars.
- Assign each student a special fish to study for an oral report.
- Use fish in an art lesson.
- Grade all papers with a set of fish stamps during "Fish Month."
- Use an overhead projector to illustrate and label parts of a fish.
- Draw a map showing where various fish are located.
- Finally, arrange a field trip to a nearby fish hatchery or aquarium.

State Departments of Fish and Game usually have booklets which are great for research.

Visit a place of historical importance Intermediate students enjoy visiting historical buildings, parks or towns after reading stories in their social science and history books. Some general ideas for such field trips include:

- Introduce the unit by teaching from an attractive bulletin board illustrating the historical site.
- Obtain hand-out materials from the local or state office of public relations.
- Draw historical maps.
- Design posters on the history of the area, including a timeline.
- Do research in the computer's encyclopedia which details the importance of your destination.
- Give oral reports.
- Carry out the grand finale—the field trip.

 EXAMPLE: A group of intermediate students visited the Alamo in San Antonio after studying Texas history. As they walked through the buildings, they observed the guns and powder used to defend the Alamo. Plan events to make lessons "come alive" for your students.

Parent helpers In order to go on field trips, you'll need adult chaperones. The number needed may vary by grade level. Check with your school office. Ask more parents than you'll need. At the last minute, parents or children get sick and you'll need a substitute.

 CAUTION: Be careful about driving your students on field trips. Some veteran teachers refuse to drive any longer. We live in a society where a lawsuit is often around the next corner. Also, check with your school office to be sure you can ask parents to drive. You must know they have a valid driver's license and insurance coverage. It's best to take a district school bus.

Call your parent helpers several days before the trip, letting them know what you expect them to do. Use the examples as starting ideas.

- First, thank each parent for joining you.
- Assign a certain number of students to each parent.
- Be sure each chaperone either knows the names of the students in his or her group, or names are pinned to younger students' clothing.

Marilyn, 59, now living in California, says "I still clearly remember a fourth-grade field trip to 'Old Ironsides' in Boston Harbor."

Field trips make history come alive for your students.

These days you may find that energetic grandparents are willing to help.

If you don't have a cell phone, try to recruit a parent with one.

On long trips, ask students to do a graph of the number of white horses, red barns and/or yellow trucks seen.

Take a duplicate emergency list with you.

- Ask parents to see that all their students go to the bathroom and get a drink before getting on the bus—at both ends of the trip.
- Specify that parents check to be sure each child has brought lunch and a drink.
- Ask parents to check students' bags to be sure all necessary items such as pencil, eraser, crayons and paper are there.
- If going some distance, ask a parent to bring a cooler for carrying cold drinks for the class.
- Designate an adult to be in charge of any snacks you have.
- Tell parents where you want them to sit on the bus.
- Ask chaperones to come at least 15 minutes early to get last-minute instructions, as needed.
- Let parents know that they are to make sure each child in their group behaves.
- Promptly write a thank-you note to each chaperone after the trip or have your students do this as part of a language lesson.

Teacher responsibility You will also have specific things you'll need to do before the trip. Your list might include:

- Notify the cafeteria manager that your class will be on a field trip on a specific date.
- If you have students on free lunch, ask to have their cafeteria bag lunches and milk ready 20 minutes before you leave.
- Provide the office with a class list and names and phone numbers of their parents in case of emergency.

The day before On the day before your field trip, do a practice "run through."

- Give each student a grocery bag to mark with his or her name, plus a small plastic bag to fill with crayons, eraser and pencil.
- Provide 12" x 12" chalkboards to serve as students' desks.
- Give each student an individual folder with worksheets about the field trip.
- Review classroom rules, and stress that they are in force on trips.
- Have students select partners for the trip.
- Students need to learn the names of parents who will be responsible for them.
- Divide your class into small groups to assign bus seating; those in the front at the beginning, ride in back to return.

As an art lesson, ask your students to design their own name tags.

- Remind students to bring snacks, lunches or drinks. Show them the labeled boxes you'll use to carry the food.
- Announce the time that the bus will leave. Explain that a fellow teacher will take any students into his or her room for the day if they miss the bus.
- Remind students that they must visit the restroom and get a drink before boarding the bus—both going and returning.
- Remind students to get plenty of rest and to wear comfortable clothes and shoes for the trip.
- Assign two students to bring some P.E. equipment to use at rest stops and during the lunch break.
- Tell students they may each bring one small, *quiet* toy to play with on the bus.
- Use your cell phone to alert the school office if you'll be delayed and ask them to notify your students' parents.

Plan a couple of quiet songs to sing as you travel along.

TEACHER TIP: *Overplan your field trips. If you don't have a steady stream of activities, you'll find the noise level can increase with every mile. Remind students the school bus is exactly like a classroom except it has wheels! By planning ahead, you'll ensure that your students and parent helpers will have an enjoyable and informative day. And so will you!*

On the day Use your checklist so you don't forget anything.
- Make sure you have a cooler for drinks.
- Bring along a First Aid Kit.

Call ahead and ask your guide to use a mike or borrow yours so all can hear the presentation.

- If available, use a portable microphone (check its batteries before you leave!) to give instructions on the trip.
- Bring extras such as tissues for runny noses; and pencils, crayons, erasers and paper for lessons on the bus.
- Wear your most comfortable shoes and bring coffee and a nutritious snack for yourself to keep up your energy level.
- Bring along extra coffee, paper cups and cookies to share with your parent helpers.

♣ HINT: On field-trip day, your students will often come to school absolutely "revved." Many will have had little sleep the night before. They'll be anxious to get going and swear they don't need to use the bathroom. Insist that they visit anyway.

The day after Allow time for final wrap-up on the day following your field trip. Ask students to finish and then share their artwork and written work assigned on the trip. Ask questions about two new things they learned and what was the most enjoyable part of the overall experience.

Fund Raisers

With school districts in short supply of money, you may need to raise funds in order to take your class on even one field trip. The thought of this turns many people cold, but if your district allows you to raise money, you can turn your "Fund Raisers" into "Fun Raisers" by putting a little amusement into the project.

♣ HINT: Ask your school office if homemade foods are permitted at school fund raisers.

Renting a bus for a long trip can be expensive. Plan ahead.

- In September, send a letter to all parents listing your needs. For example: We need money to rent a bus.
- Be explicit: I need each parent to donate two dozen homemade cupcakes for a bake sale, parents to work at stated times and an overall parent supervisor.

It pays to advertise You must let ALL the students at school know you're going to hold a bake sale. Here's how:

- Have students design posters to put up a week before the sale.
- If your students are too young, ask for help from intermediates.
- Have a student make a sandwich board for you or students to wear at recess and lunch hour.
- Teach your students to sing a jingle as you all march around the school with the board.

- Invite other students on the playground to march and sing with you.

Classroom Speakers

Field trips take your students into their community. Classroom speakers bring the community into your classroom. Use them often.

Sources Good speakers come from a variety of places.

- Many of your children's parents have hobbies or careers of interest.
- Keep your ears open for potential speakers at parties, family gatherings and other social functions.
- Invite local television weatherpersons if you're doing a weather unit.
- Radio talk shows often interview suitable local guests.
- Call the Public Affairs Officer of a nearby military base or your local Armed Forces recruiting office for speakers.
- Local police or fire departments like to send officers to schools to explain safety.
- Health-agency personnel can tell what they do and recommend ways to help keep us healthy.
- Local businesspersons who work in places like bakeries or auto or bait shops can tell how their work helps us.
- Staff from your local library or park are happy to explain their resources.
- Invite parents and grandparents to come to school and enjoy the speaker.

Your retired uncle may be an entomologist (bug man) who would enjoy sharing his beetle collection.

NOTE: Some speakers ask for a sum of money to come and speak. If needed, ask another classroom to join with you to help defray the expenses.

Publicity for your classroom speakers If you have room for guests, use the school newspaper, flyers to be sent home, telephone calls, community newspapers and the public service forum on television.

HINT: If your school has a Web site on the Internet, place an announcement on the Web about your speaker.

Class preparation Make the class as knowledgeable as possible before your speaker comes.

- Put up a bulletin board illustrating the speaker's topic.
- Invite the class to write questions to mail to the speaker before the visit.
- Prepare the class with a list of vocabulary words on your guest's topic.

Speaker preparation Touch bases ahead of time with your speaker so you're both prepared for the big day.

- Reconfirm the date and time ten days before the visit.
- Tell the speaker the time allotted to the presentation and encourage bringing exhibits.
- Ask if you need equipment such as a projector.
- Assure the speaker you and your students are looking forward to the program.
- Send a map showing how to get to your school.
- Inform the office you're expecting a speaker.

> Many schools have students who design and update school Web sites. Recruit one to advertise for you.

After the presentation Follow-up activities enhance the speaker experience.

- Have your class write individual thank-you letters to the speaker.
- Remind them to write something personal in their notes such as, "I especially liked the green beetle you brought."
- Have each student draw a picture about the lesson.
- For the letters and art make a cover with the speaker's name, your school name and the date.
- Follow up with a thank-you phone call within three days of the presentation.

We've been talking about adult speakers, but now I also must share the joys of using peer speakers in your classroom. As an example, I've worked for several years with my intermediate students teaching them to write stories on the computer. Most are becoming quite proficient. Yet, in each class, I have two or three outstanding, budding artists with great talent which is often overlooked. We need to devote more time and energy to these creative artisans. These youngsters can speak to your class about drawing comic figures, illustrating a poem or designing a greeting card.

Remember that a person doesn't have to be an adult to have special skills, abilities or interests. Many young students in our classrooms have a variety of hobbies such as building model airplanes, designing computer software or playing a musical instrument.

One way to counter our "buy-buy" society is to have classroom youngsters share their special talents with others. At least some of these speakers will undoubtedly awaken your students' inner artistic selves.

Some question ideas for your peer presenters might be:

- Explain and demonstrate the procedures to illustrate a story or a book.
- Detail the steps you follow to draw a comic strip.
- Show the steps to design a Web site.

Questions to pose to the young speaker:

- How old were you when you began your hobby?
- What kind of training have you had?
- What materials do you need to do your work?

"It's sad when we seem to be training youngsters to be super-duper buyers of tomorrow (mostly plastic) instead of teaching them to build, design or draw some of their own products."

An elementary teacher

Ask a youngster who draws comic figures to come to your classroom. This might be someone in your class or a nearby middle school.

Nothing speaks more loudly to students than to see a peer succeeding in a special field.

- Have you ever sold any of your art products or services?
- Name two books you would suggest that students might read to understand how to illustrate, to do comic strips, or to design a Web site.

 HINT: Set aside a bulletin board where the student speaker can showcase his/her work.

When introducing your peer speaker, consider that you might be giving your students a hobby for life. Specialties to consider are growing earthworms, stamp collecting, photography or cake decorating.

While your students may not all be interested in a particular hobby, the message delivers the importance of leisure activities and the many satisfactions gained from pursuing them.

Today many of our students have had little or no opportunity to experience outside activities. Through your teaching, you can open up a whole new world to them. Use field trips and the shared responsibility to help pay their cost, as well as outside and peer speakers, to add valuable enrichment experiences for your class.

Paperwork

We are living in an information society. The world is filled with memos, bulletins and "little yellow stickies." Most schools have forms for everything from bathroom passes to requests for video and computer software. Since your classroom is a mini-corporation, you must quickly get a handle on simplifying and managing your paperwork.

Some fortunate teachers have a classroom computer for tracking attendance, printing parent notices and delivering report cards. However, for many teachers, "high-tech" is only now becoming available.

This chapter will outline the typical classroom paperwork divided into daily, weekly, monthly, quarterly, yearly and ongoing segments. The sample forms may not look exactly like yours, but in most cases the purpose is the same.

Daily paperwork
- Mark students in class register.
- Complete lunch form.
- Discuss daily calendar.
- Record absence excuses and tardy notices.
- Check on academic/behavior contracts.

♣ HINT: To help with the paper blitz, go to your teacher bookstore and purchase gradebook software. The program includes a page for each student, a page for grades and space for comments.

Blizzard control:
- Have a specific place to file each form.
- A rack/hanger near the door holds hall passes.
- Safeguard computer disks in special containers.

Feel free to make copies of this chapter and file each section into a special color-coded folder in your desk. List the forms on the outside of each folder.

Weekly paperwork

- Complete lesson plans.
- Write Monday Memo (note to parents).
- Send weekly reports home on some students.
- Write out notices for missed homework.
- Note Student-of-the-Week.

Monthly paperwork

- Post yard- and bus-duty charts.
- Complete class register or computer form for office.
- Provide office with absence/tardy notes.
- Pass out P.T.A. Newsletter to students.
- Each month, or when a student leaves, update your seating chart.

Quarterly or trimester paperwork

- Send home deficiency notices.
- Fill out report cards/Parent-Conference forms.
- Complete a permanent-record form after each report-card period.
- Fill out reading, language and math charts.
- Order films, CDs, videos and computer software.

Yearly paperwork

- Prepare a substitute folder.
- Post the yearly, district school calendar.
- Present the office with an emergency card for each student. To be valid, a parent must sign it.
- Send home early/late reading times if you're on this schedule.
- Provide a notice to parents regarding your homework policy.
- Send home the parent handbook containing the school's rules the first month of school.
- Complete an end-of-year card on each student in June, stating reading and math levels and behavior.
- Give the basic achievement tests mandated by your state.
- Issue retention forms to students repeating the grade.
- Post minimum-day, snowy-day and rainy-day schedules.
- Send out parent-volunteer forms.
- Place requests for all field trips and have available field-trip permission forms.
- Have forms for free and reduced lunch.

Some forms must be done in duplicate. Or triplicate. Quadruplicate, even! Be sure you can read the last copy.

Ongoing paperwork

- Class list: update frequently for school and your home.
- Update telephone numbers of parents.
- File new-student forms.
- Complete transfer forms.
- Send notes to parents of students having problems.
- Send reminder forms to parents, if your office doesn't, to those who fail to write absence notes.
- Give grade-level tests in reading, language and math.
- Keep a portfolio file of students' writing projects.
- Have office and nurse passes available.
- When on an exchange program, keep anecdotal notes and grades to pass on to your fellow teacher for report cards.
- Keep samples of students' work to show at Open House and Parent Conferences.

TEACHER TIP: Attend workshops in your area on classroom management, read articles in teachers' magazines on handling paperwork, visit teacher Web sites on the Internet and ask veteran teachers how they manage.

District Supplemental Help

Your district may have available booklets which should help you in the classroom.

Course of study A useful one will detail a year's *course of study,* listing *specific* objectives in *specific* subjects for *specific* grade levels.

It's important to follow your district's curriculum guides as well as your basic texts. This way your students won't miss important skills they'll need as they move up the grades.

Resource units Another booklet offered by many districts describes activities and resources designed to help teachers prepare special teaching units. These units are usually prepared by groups of teachers and offer excellent alternatives from which you can select.

Starting a week with no lesson plan is like starting a trip with no map.

Lesson Plans

The more you're able to plan successful lessons across the curriculum units and interrelated projects, the more self-assured you'll feel as a teacher. By planning your lessons for each day, you'll minimize the start of behavior problems. You'll lead your students toward definite, stated goals. Always overplan, especially the first year. For additional information on lesson plans on the Internet, see Chapter 17, Technology in the Classroom.

TEACHER TIP: Never throw out your lesson-plan book at the end of the year, even if you're going to be teaching at another grade level. You never know when you'll need it again. Use it as a resource for planning your curriculum, ordering videos and providing field-trip ideas for the next year.

One great idea used by many teachers is to color code lesson plans. For example, all yard-duty times could be red, assemblies blue and recess periods in green. When showing a video, draw a little video box on the plan and a film when showing films.

Emergency Card

These important cards, to be completed by parents, go home the first week of school. When they're returned, be sure all information is listed and a parent has signed.

Before turning in the cards to the office, either write down or put into your computer all parents' names, home addresses and telephone numbers. Make one copy to keep in your desk and one to take home.

During the year, keep the office informed of changes on cards such as new addresses, telephone numbers and care providers.

Class Register

You may keep attendance on a school register or on computer forms. If you're using the school register, take it outside with you for fire drills. Always keep it in a safe place.

On the register you must record students who enter, leave, are absent or are tardy. At a specific time each month, this information goes to the office.

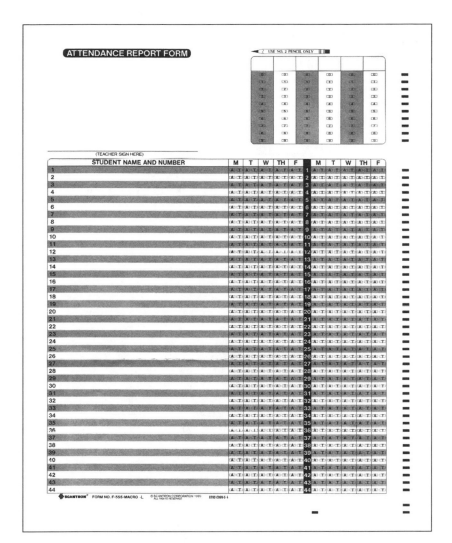

If you're using a school computer, make back-up disks at least once a week and keep them at home. Computers are often targeted by thieves or vandals.

Substitute Folder

At the beginning of the year, be sure to prepare a substitute folder in case you're absent.

 SUGGESTION: Pick out a bright red folder and print in bold letters, "Sub Folder: Welcome!"

Inside the folder you should have the following:

- An up-to-date seating plan of your classroom
- An information sheet giving the daily schedule, telling where lesson plans are kept, giving the morning's opening procedure, explaining your management system, listing your reading groups and naming the teacher next door to answer any questions

Absence-Verification Form

This is a small form which is usually sent home by the teacher if an absent student returns to school without a written excuse. If the form is not returned, the office staff will often phone the home. Check with your school secretary to see if you need this form.

SCHOOL DISTRICT
PETER BURNETT ELEMENTARY SCHOOL
Absence Verification

Date: _____

Student Name: _____

Room # Teacher: _____ Grade ____

Dates Of Absence(s): _____

_____

Reason Of Absence(s)

_____ Illness, Dr./Appt.
_____ Death In Family
_____ Out Of Town/ Vacation
_____ Personal Business (court, legal, etc.)
_____ Other (please specify) _____
_____
_____

Designee Signature
Verified By: Parent, Principal, Teacher, School Community
Liaison, Secretary, Other_____
(Circle One)

Permanent-Record Form

As students enter your school, permanent-record forms will be coded for them and placed in the permanent-record folders at your school site. This form will follow each student in your classroom through his or her school days. Guard it carefully.

After each report-card period, you'll need to enter grades, days of attendance and subject levels. You'll also record the date, the student's grade and the names of parent or parents who attended each Parent Conference. At picture time, you'll be given a small individual picture of each of your students. This picture should be pasted on the form found in the permanent record.

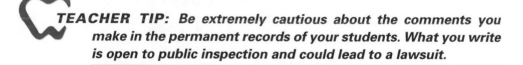

TEACHER TIP: *Be extremely cautious about the comments you make in the permanent records of your students. What you write is open to public inspection and could lead to a lawsuit.*

Deficiency Notice

Usually about three weeks before report cards are scheduled to go home, you'll notify parents of any students doing below-"C" level in schoolwork or citizenship. You may choose to send deficiency notices home with the child or mail them to the home to be signed and returned to you.

➥ NOTE: Don't forget to file a copy of the notice into the student's permanent folder.

Report Cards

Depending upon your school schedule, students will receive report cards three or four times a year. The card indicates the progress the youngster is making in class. Some schools use report cards while others use computer cards. A copy of the report card should be placed in the student's permanent file folder in the office.

Children differ in interest and ability. They differ in the rate at which they grow mentally and physically. Children need continual encouragement and guidance. The progress of your child is evaluated by teacher judgment and objective means. The purpose of this report is to accurately reflect the child's mental, physical, and social growth this year. Although the skills listed represent your child's level of performance in relation to grade level standards at this time, there is no optimum level since children develop at different rates. The skills listed are the outcome of our integrated holistic approach to the curriculum and are not taught in isolation.

SPECIAL PROGRAM PARTICIPATION

CHECKED (✓) IF APPLICABLE	1st Tri	2nd Tri	3rd Tri
Bilingual			
Chapter 1/SCE			
GATE			
Resource Program			
Speech/Language			

SCHOOL YEAR 19___ / _____

ATTENDANCE	1st Tri	2nd Tri	3rd Tri
Days Tardy			
Days Absent			
Date of Enrollment _____			

GRADED SUBJECTS

INTEGRATED LANGUAGE ARTS

LISTENING/SPEAKING
- Understands and interprets what is said
- Organizes and presents information
- Expresses ideas clearly

READING
- Uses word attack skills
- Comprehends what is read
- Reads with expression and fluency
- Increases vocabulary

WRITING
- Develops ideas
- Writes for a variety of purposes
- Uses grammar/mechanics correctly
- Applies spelling skills to written work

MATHEMATICS
- Number
- Measurement
- Geometry
- Functions
- Statistics and Probability
- Logic and Language
- Algebra
- Discrete Mathematics

SCIENCE
- Life sciences
- Earth sciences
- Physical sciences

SOCIAL SCIENCE/HISTORY
- Grade level content
- Cultural diversity
- Geographical concepts
- Democratic and civic values

ART
HEALTH
LIBRARY
MUSIC —Classroom/Vocal
PHYSICAL EDUCATION

NON-GRADED SUBJECTS

WORK HABITS
- Follows directions/listens attentively
- Works cooperatively with others
- Works independently
- Completes assignments promptly and neatly
- Participates in class discussions
- Uses class time efficiently
- Completes homework on time

SOCIAL SKILLS
- Respects rights/property of others
- Demonstrates self-control
- Solves problems appropriately
- Observes class/school rules

1ST TRIMESTER
_____
PARENT SIGNATURE   CONFERENCE HELD

2ND TRIMESTER
_____
PARENT SIGNATURE   CONFERENCE HELD

3RD TRIMESTER
_____
PARENT SIGNATURE

YOUR CHILD IS ASSIGNED TO THE _____ GRADE FOR THE 19___ SCHOOL YEAR.

NOTE: The letters A, B, C, D, F will be given for graded subjects, and S or I for non-graded subjects in each of the major headings. The sub-headings or effort column (grey) are optional and will be marked only if they differ significantly from the major heading. An asterisk (*) indicates that assessment was done in the student's primary language.

GRADED SUBJECTS KEY		NON-GRADED SUBJECTS KEY AND WORK HABITS/SOCIAL SKILLS KEY
A = Outstanding Achievement	D = Limited Achievement	S = Successful Progress I = Improvement Needed
B = Very Good Achievement	F = Unsatisfactory Achievement	
C = Satisfactory Achievement		

The receiving teacher at the next school desperately needs this information. Do it the day the student leaves. Complete the information requested and take the folder to the office at once.

Reading Chart

In most school districts you'll be expected to record scores on some type of report for grade-level tests for reading, math and language. It's best to do this after each report-card period, especially if you're teaching in a high-transiency area. If students move, you'll have the information ready for the school office.

Desk cleanout: At least once each month, require students to clean out their desks. Provide each with a large paper bag for this project.

End-of-Year Card

At some schools, you'll be asked to record reading and math levels, pages completed in the textbook and work habits. You'll appreciate receiving this vital information each September from the preceding teacher.

Although you'll find you're responsible for much paperwork, you have helpers nearby. Assign students in your classroom to take lunch and milk count while you take a quick head count each morning and record absences.

 SUGGESTION: Make yourself a colorful "mailbox" and place it near your desk. Ask students to deposit all forms, absence notes and letters from parents in the box. Later in the morning when you have a short break, sort and file.

To keep from being inundated by paperwork, you need to initiate some of kind of organization from the beginning of the year. Make a checklist of what your own school requires and when. Then meet these deadlines and keep copies of completed forms/records (or a notation of completion) so you'll know you're meeting requirements on schedule.

Special Challenges

ally Johnson graduated from college last June with a B.S. in education. She began her teaching career in September in a fifth-grade class filled with behavior problems. Forty-two days later she left teaching, probably forever. She was "dumped on."

Sally Johnson is not her real name but her story is true. According to statistics, one-third of all teachers, usually in their first year of teaching, are "dumped on."

In education jargon this means the teacher gets more than his or her share of problem students. Sometimes fellow teachers are guilty of dumping, sometimes the principal and sometimes both.

Some teachers survive dumping their first year only to be dumped on again when changing schools or districts.

There are several ways to help avoid this unfair procedure:

- Be knowledgeable. Ask about the number of behavior-problem students placed in your classroom.

- Be up-front in your interviews and let your school district know of your concern about getting dumped on.

- As soon as you sign a contract and visit your new school, tell the principal you expect your class will not be filled with students with behavior problems.

- Select your own personal "buddy" teacher at the school to assist you.

- Ask to see the end-of-the-year cards for your classroom to see if you have been given an excessive number of behavior problems.

♣ HINT: If you should end up with a class filled with problem students, ask a colleague at your school or a mentor teacher or a peer coach for assistance. Don't "go it alone."

This chapter will discuss other special challenges you'll meet in the classroom. In each case, concrete suggestions are given for overcoming problems so you can be the successful teacher *you know* you can be.

Read this chapter carefully, make notes and jot down ideas on sticky note paper to attach to these pages for quick references as needed. Make this chapter your very own personal "Teacher First-Aid Kit." Use as required.

Topics to be covered include:

- Being the new teacher
- Teacher evaluations
- Staying healthy
- Teaching a split class
- Teaching students from other ethnic, cultural and religious backgrounds
- Substituting
- Threats
- Stress relief
- Improving your professional life

> "To give the toughest kids to a first-year teacher is really criminal."
>
> Michael McKibbin
> Project Manager
> Commision on
> Teacher Credentialing
> California

Being the New Teacher

Whether you're one of a hundred new teachers hired in a large inner-city school district or the only new face in a small mountain community, you'll be beginning an entirely new phase in your life. You can help make the transition from student to teacher as smooth as possible.

Get to know your staff Make an effort to get acquainted:

- As you pass members of the staff, smile and say a genuine, "Hello."
- Ask the secretary for the faculty list.
  - Study names.
  - Memorize room numbers for each.
  - Repeat names and their grade levels to yourself.

▪ Study the list of names and positions of support staff.

    - Cafeteria personnel

    - Custodian

    - District superintendent

    - School librarian

    - School nurse

    - School psychologist

    - School secretary

    - Speech teacher

    - Yard-duty helpers

Learn to adjust One way to adjust is to be quiet your first year. Let all the new information simply filter into your brain while you sit, listen and observe. Additional suggestions are:

▪ Don't compare yourself to others.

▪ Begin to network with other teachers at your school or elsewhere. Support is vital.

▪ Accept both your strengths and your weaknesses, while dwelling on your strengths.

▪ Give yourself permission to be a beginner and to make mistakes.

Classroom suggestions These four suggestions can help you have a good year:

▪ Remember that not every student will like you and that's OK.

▪ You shouldn't expect to "right every wrong" in your students' lives. If you try, you may burn out.

- Create a nurturing classroom for your students.
- Prepare for rainy/snowy days by doing the following:
    - Ask parents to send in games no longer used at home. Before using, have a student check that all pieces are included.
    - Visit garage sales and pick up other games and activities suitable for classroom use.
    - Purchase a book on P.E. and rainy/snowy-day activities. *Awesome P.E. Activities* by Carnes is outstanding.

Don't try to do it all by yourself One of the kindest things you can do for yourself is to ask for help. Veteran teachers have several ways to ease their workloads:

Stay organized. When teaching in the primary grades, ask an intermediate student, when available, to help you file, clean out drawers and run errands.

Correcting papers:
- An aide can correct papers.
- A parent can grade papers at home.
- You could hire a teen to come in after school and correct papers.

- Have cross-age tutors work with individual students.
- Use parental help during reading and math.

Evaluations

During your first year, your principal will evaluate your teaching several times. Things to do ahead are:

- Find out what is meant by both new and old terms such as "balanced literacy approach," "phonics and whole language" and "language development for students whose primary language is not English."
- Look at the school plan.

- Be knowledgeable about the standards for teachers in your state.
- If you have federal or state funding, note key words.
- Know and understand the teaching styles the principal considers important.
- Ask to observe a teacher using these styles.

Stay Healthy

Teaching school can be injurious to your health. One intermediate teacher had the flu three times in one year and a man who taught kindergarten caught the measles. Try not to let this happen to you!

Prepare ahead for being in a classroom often filled with children sniffling, sneezing and moping around with fevers.

Try some of these strategies that work for others:

- During the summer, ask your doctor for suggestions to keep up your resistance to germs.
- Whatever has prevented colds for you in the past, use it now.
- Eat well-balanced meals and arrange for some type of exercise several times a week. This will also help reduce stress.

To help stay healthy:
- Drink lots of water.
- Get plenty of rest.
- Wash your hands often.
- Eat properly.
- Exercise regularly.

Check to see if flu shots are covered by your health plan.

- If flu shots work for you, ask your doctor about receiving one as soon as possible.
- Keep a soap dispenser in the classroom and wash your hands often so you won't transfer cold or flu germs from others. Keep your hands away from your face, especially your eyes and lips.

Bathroom blues Teachers appear to have a high rate of bladder and kidney infections. In most cases, doctors say teachers don't take time to go to the bathroom. Teachers argue they just don't *have* time.

If finding time for the bathroom is a problem, here are three suggestions:

- Arrange with the teacher next to you to watch each other's classes, especially on rainy/snowy days, so you can take necessary breaks.
- Be sure to set your classroom timer each day to go off five minutes before recess, so you'll have your students out the door on time and you can walk to the bathroom.
- Drink extra water during the day to help you avoid bladder and kidney infections. By using preventive measures, you can go through your teaching year with a minimum of sick days.

Split Classes

You definitely shouldn't have a split class your first year of teaching, but it can happen, so be prepared. Three veteran teachers who have taught a number of splits offer some suggestions:

- You should be given students with good behavior and who can work well independently.
- If possible, try to have equal numbers from each grade level. Also, it works better to have a nearly equal number of boys and girls.
- Arrange the classroom so each grade level is together.
- Work with all the students as one group for the first week while you get your discipline and management systems up and running.
- Provide your students with many independent-work opportunities such as library books, learning centers and resources for keeping journals and doing research. This is where computers in the classroom can be most helpful.
- Don't repeat the same lessons with each group. Each level has definite skill requirements. Don't cheat them by teaching to the entire class at all times.

- Teach music, art and P.E. as one group.

- Be cautious about the way you correct the older students in front of the younger ones. The older youngsters should be treated more as young adults. Let them know they can take on more responsibility than the younger group. But, if they fail, don't make an example of them in front of the lower grade.

- You can use your older students as cross-age tutors, but don't overdo this or they'll miss out on specific skills for their own level.

- Overplan each week. Lesson plans should be done in great detail, instructions placed on chalkboard and step-by-step instructions supplied for each student doing independent work.

- Enlist parents to help run learning centers, answer questions and work along with small groups.

Students Observing Religious Requirements

You'll often discover during the first week of school that you have students who can't participate in certain classroom activities because of religious convictions or who must be away on specific days for religious observances.

NOTE: As we continue to see children coming from overseas, your classroom will become more and more diverse. Students may arrive with different religions. Differing needs can be addressed through books, plays and speakers from the local community.

There are ways to work with children from religious backgrounds at variance with school curriculum:

- Communication with parents is vital. Ask them for a conference so you can learn what their wishes are.

- Take notes.

- Ask if a new student may salute the flag. Stress that you prefer the student stand during the salute even if he or she does not participate. If this isn't acceptable to parents, decide where the student will be during the pledge.

- Ask parents if their child should leave the classroom when parties are planned or if they'll pick up the student.

- At times, other students may note these differences by asking during Class Meetings why certain students don't have to do everything the rest of the class does. Use this time to explain

Plan ahead for an interpreter if needed. If an adult is not available, you may have to ask an older student to serve as the interpreter.

the need to understand others and point out that you've prepared separate lessons for these students to do on certain days.

Students from Other Ethnic and Cultural Backgrounds

America's population is changing and we see this every day in our classroom. Some suggestions follow on how to create a classroom where learning can take place for these special students:

It's not unusual in many states, for a teacher to have students from Viet Nam, Bosnia, Mexico and Russia in the same room.

- If possible, for part of the day in your classroom, have a bilingual aide who can communicate with your non- or limited-English-speaking students.

- If no aide is available, enlist some volunteer bilingual parents for an hour or so a day.

- If none of these options is open, ask an older bilingual student to come to your classroom and serve as a cross-age tutor for an hour a day.

- Always communicate your concerns for your limited-English-speaking students with your principal.

- Ask a kindergarten or first-grade teacher for flash cards and have one of your students use them to work with a limited-English-speaking child.

- A computer in your classroom or a computer lab is ideal. Many software programs are available to help limited-English-speaking children.

CDs now have "Computer Karaoke™" sing-alongs. Each word is highlighted on the computer. This helps teach English to minority students.

- In some districts, a Newcomer School sponsored by the district is available for youngsters arriving from foreign countries.

- Finally, seek out information on district, community and church resources which are available for students. These might include clothing, food, interpreters, counseling and tutoring services.

TEACHER TIP: *Take advantage of the rich cultural background your foreign students and their parents bring to your classroom. Help these students give oral reports about the ethnic holidays they celebrate and encourage them to bring in "hands-on" items from their countries. Ask their English-speaking parents to share with your class. Many can bring in handwork, ethnic foods or share art projects. Use their talents.*

Substituting

In spite of the teacher shortages in some areas, many teachers prefer to substitute rather than work full time.

If you're a beginning sub, make yourself available each day if at all possible. Consider having business cards or a flyer printed to pass out at various schools within your school district. With your cards in hand, there are several ways to help establish yourself as a substitute teacher.

- Get a list of schools, principals, secretaries and a district map to familiarize yourself with city streets.

- Go over the names of the principal and school secretary so you can properly introduce yourself.

- Ask to meet the principal.

- Call him or her by name, introduce yourself and present your business card.

- Explain your background such as primary or intermediate teacher, or music or art major.

- Ask the principal if you might post your business card in the faculty room.

In one fast-growing area of the country, residents have passed a school bond with which the district will build 34 new schools in the next ten years.

Who substitutes?
- Retirees
- New teachers without full-time positions
- Young mothers who don't want to work full time

Networking is
everything.

- Write a note regarding your educational background and place under the card.

☞ NOTE: Many school districts have a system whereby they can cooperatively register substitutes for multiple districts. In urban areas, you can often sub in several areas. This allows a substitute to focus in on which schools are of most interest to him or her. Talk to other teachers and let them know you'd like to substitute in their district.

As you sub, enrich
your future teaching.
• Look for one new
  idea in each class
  you visit.
• Take along a camera
  and shoot pictures
  of outstanding
  bulletin boards.

If you have a problem obtaining a job, consider taking a class on job-seeking. Ask to have the local college videotape one of your lessons. If you wish to teach elsewhere in the country, go on the Internet and ask other teachers about openings.

🍎 **TEACHER TIP:** *You must realize that in some districts, being a great sub means* **not** *moving into a classroom. Many outstanding subs applying for a full-time position have been told, "You're such a good sub, we'd hate to lose you." Be aware that this could happen to you. Stand firm. Apply for each opening and, if needed, go for help either on the district level or to your teacher association.*

Students in a
substitute's class:
Guy Wire
Dusty Rhodes
Ted E. Behr
Warren Pease
Pete Moss
Barb Wire

The substitute's first-aid kit As you know after student teaching, you must always be prepared. Never is this more true than while being a substitute. There may not be any lesson plans waiting for you, and especially with older students, substitute teachers are fair game.

Be prepared by arriving at school with a large bag filled with the following items:

- An assortment of lessons geared for both primary and intermediate grades in reading, language, math, art and P.E.

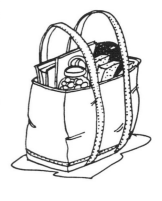

- Two or three favorite story books from your own library to read aloud. Inside the book, record the date, school and page number in case you return to that school again.
- A small bell for gaining attention.
- Your rules written on a large piece of tagboard and laminated. Post your rules as soon as you arrive in the classroom. Short, simple rules are best.

Rules in an intermediate classroom:

- Follow all directions.
- Complete your assignments.
- Ask for permission to leave the classroom.
- Always keep your hands, feet and objects to yourself.

 HINT: Be sure your students know and understand what these rules mean.

Your teaching day Let the students know you're pleased to be in their classroom and assure them you expect them to behave.

TEACHER TIP: It's best to spend 15 minutes going over your classroom rules and procedures. Otherwise, some smart-acting student will say, "But Mr. Moore doesn't do it that way. He does it this way." Immediately, several kids will yell out, "No, he does not, and you know that!"

Seating As much as possible, use the children's names by referring to the seating chart. Also, when you can immediately identify potential troublemakers, it will keep students from moving from desk to desk to confuse you.

Now that you have their attention, you're ready to follow the teacher's lesson plans or pull out your own material and begin the day.

Back-ups If you sense upon entering the school that you may have a class with behavior problems, request support from the office. Ask that the principal come to the classroom during the first hour. When the principal arrives in your room, ask him or her, in front of the students, if you can send problem students to the office. This can serve to put potential troublemakers on notice to settle down fast.

Students need to know you're there to teach and they're there to learn.

Violence and Crime

Sadly, no school is exempt from the possibility of violence and crime.

One time, while I was on yard duty, a 12-year-old student placed a homemade knife against my side and said, "I've been wanting to kill a teacher and I'm starting with you."

I was fortunate. I escaped injury, but the hard facts are that crime and violence are making their way into our nation's schools. You should take certain precautions if you're teaching in a particularly crime-prone area:

- If you don't have a telephone in your room, purchase a cell phone and keep it with you at all times.
- Find out how your police or sheriff want you to call their emergency numbers; then program your cell phone at once.
- Be on friendly terms with your teaching neighbors. Select a code you might bang on a wall if help is needed.
- Let your custodian know when you work after class dismissal and have him or her stop by to check on you.
- If working alone after the class leaves, lock your doors.
- Don't work alone in your classroom after dark.
- Try not to hold night conferences, but if you must, have another adult stay with you the entire time.
- Don't walk alone to your car in the parking lot after sundown.
- Don't hesitate to call the police if you or anyone in your class is in any personal danger at any time. Use your telephone and call 911 at once. Also, call the school office so the principal can be summoned to your room.

Know ahead of time what to do in case of an emergency such as:
• Hurricane
• Tornado
• Flood
• Earthquake
• An act of violence

Threats During my years of teaching, my students and I were once held in a locked classroom for several hours due to threats made against me to the principal.

If you're threatened in any way by a parent or student, keep your classroom doors locked during your teaching day until the problem is settled. Take all threats seriously.

Child clinical psychologist, Jonathan Kellerman, says, "My experience as a psychologist has shown me that when it comes to violence, there are few surprises. Well-adjusted kids just don't turn bad overnight. Dangerous kids spend their entire childhoods warning us."

If a student makes a threat either to you or other students, take this seriously and report it.

Domestic violence The number-one place for a spillover of domestic violence from the home is into the workplace. "What we are seeing is the perpetrator taking violence into the office, classroom or parking lot," says a California sheriff specializing in domestic violence. "The perpetrator knows exactly where the victim is each day," he adds. "This can be tragic in a classroom."

If anyone on your faculty, or a parent, is undergoing domestic violence in the home, the principal needs to know. Also, be aware of the problem that can develop in custody battles. Again, the child is in a particular room for many hours a day and a parent challenging custody can try to forcibly take the child from your room.

Stress

Teaching, like any new job, will be a series of adjustments to work, unfamiliar surroundings and new faces. Sometimes you'll feel very much alone. After all, you're usually the only adult in a classroom filled with young children. As a result, you might begin to feel "stressed out."

Signs of stress Stress can show up in any one or more of several ways:

- Frequent headaches
- Laryngitis
- Stomach problems
- Short temper
- Sleep problems
- Heart palpitations
- Sudden weight changes

Everyone may experience such symptoms from time to time, but if you get "clusters," stop to look for a pattern. It may not be stress and then you certainly should see your doctor. If it *is* stress, this is your body's way of telling you it's time to "slow down." Listen to it!

Stress relief We all share common human needs. We each need to feel we're a unique and important person. We also need to meet goals, be successful and feel good about our futures. To keep stress from taking over our lives, we must find ways to meet these human needs but not be consumed by them.

To have meaning in your life, accept yourself and find a "reason for being."

 HINT: Get a life outside the classroom. It could be the joy of reading novels, fishing, traveling or swimming. Pick an experience or activity which will last you for a lifetime. You need it now and in your retirement years.

If you suffer from stress, find ways to cut excess workload. Veteran teachers often can offer good suggestions here. Read books or magazine articles for helpful ways to decrease stress. Make time for regular exercise. For other ideas, attend stress-reduction workshops.

TEACHER TIP: *The most important word for teachers to remember is "flexibility." Make it your goal to stay calm, cool and collected even when the carpenter walks into your classroom during math to announce, "I'm gonna' replace your floor today." Take a deep breath and say, "Well, students, we're going to have another adventure this week. Let's enjoy it outside on the grass. Come, bring your chairs!"*

Improving Your Professional Life

Improving yourself in your chosen profession should be a lifetime gift to yourself. There are several ways to enhance your life as a teacher:

- Join your local, state and national organizations for teachers.
- Attend workshops to help you in areas where you feel you need to improve.
- Network with other teachers.
- Enroll in a university class.
- Read education books and journals.
- When you do something outstanding in your classroom, call your radio and television stations. Let the outside world know that you're making a positive difference in children's lives.

 CAUTION: Be careful not to attempt ideas in the classroom which are a little "off center." Both students and parents can become upset. Often, even before you leave the classroom, the news media splashes your unusual lesson across the airways and teachers are the butt of endless jokes.

Once you've finished the school year, look forward to the next. Consider, later in your career, inviting student teachers into your classroom. Be available to share and show the next generation of teachers how to be successful.

Be proud to be a teacher, for you'll touch many lives, leave a positive mark on many and have numerous opportunities to influence the future.

16

Urban and Rural Teaching

By the year 2006, two million new teachers will be hired for the nation's growing classrooms.

Why the urgent need? According to the National Education Association, skyrocketing enrollments have been brought on by growth in the immigrant population and by baby boomers' children reaching school age. At the same time, more teachers are retiring.

Major cities throughout the country are being hit hard with teacher shortages and are looking for teachers.

We need you!

In this chapter, you'll receive information on teaching in both urban and rural settings. Information comes from research and also from personal visits to urban and rural areas.

🔑 NOTE: As a future teacher, you'll have many choices for places of employment. Do your own personal research before signing a contract.

- Write for maps and information from the Chamber of Commerce.
- Subscribe to the daily newspaper for six months before deciding on "your" city or rural area.
- Visit the city or town you're considering and talk to people in the community.
- Check on the Internet for jobs and desirability of locations.
- Attend job fairs if you see them advertised.

Job fairs These days, many districts sponsor job fairs to recruit teachers. You'll have a chance to learn more about individual schools without visiting each one separately.

Although it's a "fair," never show up in jeans and jogging shoes. Dressing professionally could tip the scales toward getting the job you want.

Arrive early—there may be lines—and be ready. Have plenty of clean copies of a well-prepared resume including:

- Related experience
- Multi-lingual capability
- Letters of reference
- Telephone numbers of previous employers

Generally, you'll want to apply for jobs for which you're qualified and which represent your talents.

Urban Teaching

Teaching in an urban district Why would you choose to teach in a large urban school district? Some of the reasons are given by a consultant who works each day with new teachers in a large metropolitan district.

- For the challenge of meeting the needs of a diverse group of learners
- To assist and work with students who are different from you
- To be an important person in a child's life by offering stability, a caring attitude and a light to the future

Reasons not to go to an urban school:

- You need a job.
- You believe you'll change the world.
- You feel sorry for the students.

Who's going into teaching?
- Grandparents who were "downsized" by their companies
- Scientists who were laid off
- Early retirees from the military

"Teaching is a venue where you can turn service into a career."

Arthur Levine,
President
Teachers College, NY

We want you! Large school districts are using unique methods for attracting new teachers. One district in the south invites prospective teachers to visit a classroom for one week. While in the city, the teacher stays with a teacher who retired from the area.

Another district, with a large Spanish-speaking population, offers a generous signing bonus to bilingual teachers. Fast-growing Las Vegas recruits over the Internet and once people are hired, the district is determined to keep them. Picnics on the desert, special days honoring teachers and door prizes are offered. What urban districts look for in teachers:

- Competence
- Top training
- Energy and enthusiasm
- Desire and experience to work with inner-city students

More teachers are looking for jobs in urban areas. This is due to:

- Teacher satisfaction is increasing.
- Salaries are improving.
- Teachers are feeling more respect.

More and more older people are also joining the ranks of new teachers. They've often carved out a busy lifestyle in the corporate world and now wish to "give back."

- They believe they can make a difference in the world.
- They hope to help promote a return to values.

Dual language for bilingual students Many bilingual students live in urban areas. At the same time, questions are being asked as to whether bilingual programs are worthwhile.

However, in Chicago a program called "dual language" is being used with three- and four-year-olds in a number of schools.

These "little people" are in classrooms where they are taught Spanish for half the day and English for the remainder. Teachers in the program use body language, story books, field trips and hands-on activities to teach the children. In the next five years, the program will be expanded through the third grade.

Parent involvement Along with the "dual-language" program, Chicago schools are also reaching out to parents to serve on local school councils. Minority parents are urged to take part. The call is being heard, as more than 50 percent of the councils involve African-Americans; Hispanic parents make up 14 percent of the boards.

Urban schools need more, better-prepared teachers.

It's important to earn a living while making a difference in children's lives.

An IBM executive, once high on the corporate ladder, is now a primary teacher.

"I want to help solve problems in this country, not keep locking up people in jail."

Retired police officer
Now a teacher

Between 25 and 35 percent of people in teaching had another career first.

Studies of children's brains indicate the best time to teach a second language is before youngsters are ten years old.

In a large district in California, grandparents are invited to attend "Coffee Connections" at an urban school. Here they are honored as grandparents and as caregivers for their grandchildren. A special speaker discusses care and support issues of interest to the attendees.

Teaching in the inner-city Inner-city schools often have a diverse minority population. In order to succeed, you must join in with the community to learn about their cultures, goals for their children and the structures of their families.

As you work in the community, you must gain the parents' confidence. It's vital that you convince them of the importance of working with their children from a very early age. This means playing finger games, singing and reading to their babies and talking to them constantly. For more information on parent involvement, see Chapter 18.

Hector Dubon, principal at Wilmington Park Elementary in Los Angeles says, "Inner-city school kids come to kindergarten at age five, and they know very little compared to kids who come from affluent areas, where the parents teach them the alphabet and social skills."

Classroom management Even if you can help toward youngsters' preparation for school, you *must* have an outstanding discipline and management system to stay in the profession for the long haul.

You must be *firm* yet *fair* in your teaching. Read my chapter, Classroom Management, and reflect on it many times before you go into the classroom.

You *must* have rules, you *must* have limits and you *must* be consistent at all times.

When teachers leave, they list the overwhelming amount of time spent on classroom management as a major reason for leaving.

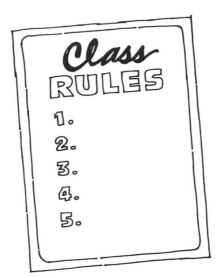

You need to empower students to be the best they can be.

♣ HINT: Look in the Bibliography for books which are helpful with classroom management.

Computers More and more classrooms have not just one, but several computers. These are an excellent resource for students to use at a Learning Center where they can do both remedial and enrichment work and discover the joys of writing a letter, report or a poem.

Downtown resources Call the Chamber of Commerce for booklets on resources for your students. These could be outstanding field trips to museums, art galleries, large bookstores and parks. Some urban areas lend themselves to walking trips for a class. Be sure students are well-supervised, and the office has been notified and necessary permission slips collected.

More and more cities, such as Denver, Colorado, have a "Jolly Trolley" which takes people on long field trips around the city at a reasonable price. Jump on a trolley with a picnic basket in tow and open up the community to your students.

To stay in the profession for the long haul, you must have a life outside the classroom. Check the Chamber of Commerce resources for ideas you will truly enjoy. These might be amateur sports, group music participation, cultural activities to attend, or some other special hobby. Whatever you choose, make sure you participate often. You'll be a happier and more effective teacher, both in the classroom and outside.

Rural Teaching

The setting Located not far from the Pacific Ocean, the long narrow valley sits isolated from the outside world.

The old school building spreads out at one end of the valley along a narrow, rural road with a stream nearby. Each day 200 elementary students head for the school, mostly on big yellow school buses.

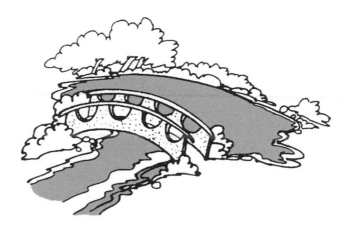

In the small faculty room, the staff table with a few chairs stands against one wall, while in the nearby cafeteria, students eat their chicken burritos for lunch.

Teachers leave keys in the ignition of their cars out in the parking lot, and their homes unlocked. "We know whenever strangers come through here," says one veteran teacher. "We could catch them before they ever made it to the main highway."

Nearby is an old country store where people lounge around visiting while sipping cold drinks. Across the street, the newest business, a pizza parlor, opened in a mobile home. It's a small world from out of the past.

The advantages of teaching in a rural area Not all rural areas are as small as the one just described. But according to surveys taken at a number of rural schools, both teachers and parents agree that the advantages outweigh the disadvantages.

- In a rural area you'll have more sense of community.

- There's more support from parents.

- There are fewer urban issues such as drugs and gangs.

- New teachers are welcomed and encouraged on the staff.

The school is the social hub for:
- Basketball games
- Plays and dramas
- Potlucks

- The teacher often knows every student and his or her family.
- There are usually fewer behavior problems.

Caring teachers Veteran teachers constantly look out for new teachers. They suggest good books to read aloud in class, they'll take problem students and work with them and offer to drive you home when your car won't start.

Not only do they care about new teachers, but they also love their students. One teacher said, "I want to stay in this community and grow old. I want to watch my students grow up here, graduate from school, marry and watch their little ones grow up."

The disadvantages of teaching in a rural area
The isolation of the school can create problems, especially for new teachers.

- Classes at the nearest university are often hours away.
- You may have to log onto the Internet to take them.
- There are usually no student or mentor teachers.
- Not many stores are available for shopping.
- There's rarely a teacher bookstore.
- It's often difficult to get substitutes.
- Falling enrollments provide less money to spend at the school.

The family/community structure In many rural communities, farmers employ minority workers for crop work. These families, often Hispanic, move on when the fall work is done. They travel to other states, or to Mexico, to work and return to the community in time for the spring planting.

Some children in these families miss weeks or months of school. Many school districts struggle to find the best way to serve these youngsters. In some areas, a migrant program is used to provide services for these intermittent students.

In some rural areas, businesses are actively recruited to move into the community and provide permanent jobs so families need not move. In one small Oregon community, two factories have moved in and are now hiring permanent workers, allowing students to regularly attend school.

The churches are also active in helping members of the community. Ministers do grief counseling and greet the gatherings of people at graduations; church members often furnish kits which include paper, pencils and other supplies for needy students.

Journal topic in one intermediate classroom: "My Favorite Place in the Valley"

By 2010, Hispanics will be the largest minority population in the United States.

TEACHER TIP: *If you're teaching in a rural community, watch your talk. If you eat out, for example, and speak about a problem concerning a student in your class, his cousin may be eating in the next booth! The word will spread rapidly—maybe even before you get home.*

The church provides food and clothing for needy families.

Much of your teaching satisfaction will depend upon the area where you feel most comfortable. Some teachers love being in urban areas with lots of people and sophisticated activities. Others don't like living in such an impersonal atmosphere. They feel more satisfied where they can know and care about their neighbors. They're happy with small-town and "simple" activities. Keep your personal preferences and the differences in mind as you choose between urban and rural teaching.

Technology in the Classroom

Maria, a kindergartner, sits crosslegged on a tall chair, gazing at a large, orange cat prancing across the computer screen. She leans over and types "c-a-t" with her right-index finger while putting the thumb of her left hand into her mouth.

Then she pulls out her thumb, looks up and smiles at me and says, "I looove computers."

Why technology in the classroom? Students at all grade levels enjoy working with computers and when used properly, this is another effective way of learning. But while computers probably represent some of the more spectacular and most common newer classroom technology, they certainly aren't the only representatives.

Technology is evolving every day. Your school probably uses at least some of the innovations which include television, cable TV, VCRs, camcorders, digital cameras, laser players, computers, Internet connections, Local Area Networks, Wide Area Networks, Liquid Crystal Displays (LCDs), CD-ROMs and more.

Research shows technology in the classroom helps students:

- Work more efficiently
- Focus on assignments

A new technology product is introduced every seven minutes.

- Feel comfortable using tools that are now commonplace
- Assume some control of their learning

When should technology use begin? ASAP! Begin in kindergarten when, for example, you take your students to visit a nearby fire station. Back at school, have your class each write a thank-you note with illustrations.

Model use of a fax machine and have the youngsters punch in the numbers, wait for the "send signal" and send their thank-you messages.

Computers in the Classroom

My first experience with computers was the morning I rolled a computer into my classroom on a cart. The trick was to schedule 31 eager third graders for our two-week turn with it.

We teachers, and computers, have come a long way since then.

Where to place computers While early school use of computers was largely confined to portable units on carts and sometimes computer labs, today more computers are being placed permanently in classrooms.

➖➤ NOTE: If your students go to a lab, it's important that you go with them. You need to know what they're doing and coordinate your classroom activities with the lab work.

Before placing computers in your classroom, plot their locations on paper. Placement will be dictated by electric and phone connections. Have the screens in view so students aren't tempted to play when they should be working.

Computers, along with proper guidance, can support the learning process in your classroom in several ways:

- Through direct instruction
- For remediation
- As a tool for research
- To express creative ideas or thoughts
- To help teach English to non-English-speaking students

➖➤ NOTE: You may not have the money or desire to place your students on the Internet but you may wish to use computers. I used computers with my primary students for several years and simply tested them on reading, math and language and placed them on the correct level of software in these subjects with outstand-

---

Sidebar notes:

Only one student arrived late for computer time.

Before hooking up computers, be sure you have a goal in mind for their use.

It's OK to be a beginner.

There's little evidence that computers will replace quality teachers.

ing results. You can do the same. Teacher bookstores, computer stores and catalogs are showing more and more software for both primary and intermediate students to go along with the subjects you're teaching.

Word processing In the primary grades, we teach students to write words, phrases and sentences. We also model for them how to write a paragraph. By the time they reach the intermediate grades, they're able to write stories and are ready to use a

computer to mix, edit and change words into a proper story, report or letter. This is when word processing is a big help to them. With a computer and a printer, they can write a report, edit, cut or move a paragraph and print a good-looking product.

Prior to introduction of a writing program, show the videos *Introduction to Computers and Windows for Kids* to familiarize your class with computer use. Then have them available for small groups for additional viewing and discussion.

Introduction to Computers comes with a learning disk. *Windows for Kids* teaches *Windows* operation and also may give instruction on how to play Minesweeper® and Solitaire, which students will love on a rainy day. For more information on these videos, go to www.viagrafix.com.

Provide for your students the joy of writing and printing their own books.

Word processing begins with text—from an interview with another student or someone in the community, from books or from the Internet.

As you prepare for word processing, take time to discuss with the class how to interview, to write and edit on the computer and how to perform the actual processes on the computer.

An outstanding program to help here is *The Student Writing Center*, by The Learning Company of Cambridge, MA. This is the company which gave us *Reader Rabbit*™ and *Math Muncher*.™

This is also the time to present a list of glossary words and definitions pertinent to word processing. Ask students to use classroom resources to add ten more computer-related, defined words to share with the class.

Glossary words:
• Clip art
• Menu bar
• Pulldown menu
• Cursor
• Default
• Double click
• Filename
• Paste
• Retrieve
• Window

Another piece of outstanding software to assist with word processing is *ClarisWorks*® by the Claris Corporation. To establish your own firm foundation in word processing, read *ClarisWorks*® *for Terrified Teachers* by Terry Rosengart. The author explains how to insert graphics, how to outline, insert materials and much more. It's a great resource for you and your students to use. It should be available at your local teacher store.

While individual ability to use the computer is necessary, writing reports and doing word processing projects also provide students with the opportunity to work together in cooperative groups. Through the collaborative process, they should pick one student to be the editor, another the illustrator and another the word processor. Roles should be traded after a predetermined time.

Some students now produce their own school newspaper.

By third grade, all students should be on a typing program. *Mavis Beacon Teaches Typing* is an outstanding software program.

For more ideas on word-processing projects, see *Writing and Desktop Publishing on the Computer* by Terry Rosengart.

Multimedia—What Is It?

Multimedia is the use of more than one medium for a project. For example, a student might do a photo essay of a field trip, using a camera or camcorder for pictures to accompany his written or oral report. Computers aren't essential for a successful multimedia project, but they can help students create reports on word processors for their presentation with pictures, sounds or movies.

Teachers are no longer the sole gatekeepers of information.

John Roberts,
Teacher
Sacramento, CA

Today students work together with powerful technology tools.

Multimedia might include use of a scanner and utilization of a word-processor person, a graphic artist and a video director.

❖ HINT: To integrate technology into your classroom:

- Plan.
- Plan.
- Plan ahead.

A good resource for use of multimedia is *Multimedia Projects* by Deborah Shepherd Hayes.

We observe class-mates teaching each other.

The Internet for Research and Communication

While computers and other media offer invaluable learning help to students, addition of the Internet enhances the process even more. It opens up whole new worlds. The Internet is a shared system with others and the word means "interactivity."

E-mail Many people consider e-mail to be the most important tool on the Internet. It enables both primary and intermediate students to write to other students all over the world. Before they begin, take time to discuss the rules and procedures for writing pen pals by e-mail. Some topics to address with your students are:

- Write the pal at least once a week.
- Write three questions about a reading, math or science lesson you're working on.
- Explain what you're studying in school.

NOTE: Your students' pen pals should be acquired from Web sites that are recognized as leaders in education. A good example is the Global Schoolhouse which has a pen-pal exchange at www.k12.cnidr.org/gsh/gshwelcome.html.

Internet for Kids talks about e-mail, discusses "Netiquette" and introduces URLs. For more information on this video, go to www.viagrafix.com.

Virtual schools Virtual schools are becoming more common, particularly for students in remote areas or in hospitals. Here students work on computers to receive and complete their lessons. Usually each student works under the supervision of a teacher who may have 30 other students. The student obtains information on lessons, does research or participates in "real-time" discussion groups monitored by the teacher.

In turn, the student sends homework by e-mail or fax to the teacher.

URL stands for "Uniform Resource Locator." This is an address that tells your Web browser which page to display.

The virtual school provides a server that allows students access to stored information.

Build for the future—this is where it is.

Video conferencing Video conferencing is being used more and more by students in classrooms. Even third graders enjoy use of this medium. The immediacy of occasionally interacting with famous people or subject experts really gets students excited about learning. For more information go to www.gsn.org/cu/index.html, which is the Global SchoolNet Foundation, and click on cu-SeeMe.

The Global SchoolNet site aims to stimulate creative thinking and create a wide base of user experiences. Teachers can obtain lesson plans for interactive video activities here as well.

TEACHER TIP: With little money for field trips, the Internet becomes a field trip for your students. One student may e-mail a friend in Ireland while another might visit a Web site and look at historical ruins in Italy for a social studies report. The Internet also becomes a powerful tool to motivate a reluctant classroom student to learn.

Using the Web Because of the multitude of different Web sites on the Internet, many "Net-generation" students are no longer willing to sit passively in front of the television watching the same old sitcoms. Instead, they prefer to interact with fellow students in South Africa or elsewhere and talk about what each had for breakfast and what was studied at school that day.

Young people on the "Net" have developed their own rules, and "Netiquette" lets others online know when they've overstepped the boundaries of good taste. In monitored chat rooms, on-line misbehavior can get a visitor ejected or even blocked from the room. People suspect, however, that unmonitored bad behavior will prompt legislation from adults to limit children's access to the Net.

NOTE: Before you recommend a site to a student or parent, preview it yourself to know its content and appropriateness.

Girls by the age of 11 enjoy going online and into chat rooms, while boys join, on average, at age 13. They leave messages for each other, talk with students in other countries and gain knowledge beyond their homes and classrooms.

One frequently used student site is the Seattle-based Free Zone with the Web address, www.freezone.com. The colorful page has a "he said/she said" section, another for Brainstorming and one for the Kulture Club. Young people leave messages with signatures such as Skoop, Phoenix, wowme and Pookee.

Most sites have links to other outstanding Web sites.

Students on line:
• Enjoy chatting
• Make new friends
• Obtain information
• Enjoy learning a
  new way

The Internet may become the field trip of the future.

Some chat rooms are "rude and crude." Teachers need to monitor their use.

Warn your students to *never* give out personal information in a chat room.

Designing Web sites While "cruising" the Internet, you'll discover a number of student-designed Web sites for schools. These might include the school's name and location, a drawing of the school mascot, a list of coming events, even the lunch menu.

ClarisWorks® software includes instructions for designing Web sites.

More and more students are being taught to design their own and school Web pages. An outstanding model you can view is the Matsuyama Elementary School in Sacramento, California, at www.mes.room.net.

While constructing a Web site, students write for a purpose, learn to design a home page and develop graphic skills. Once the site is operating, they monitor it for messages and number of "hits." A hit occurs when someone visits a site. Some popular sites may have thousands of hits a day.

You can obtain a hit counter on the Net. Do a word search on "hit counters" and you can download the counter.

 HINT: Claris Works® is a good program for students to use for page layouts, clip art and for stationery and flier designs.

For outstanding information on the future generation of technology students, read *Growing up Digital, The Rise of the Net Generation* by Don Tapscott. The author has conducted an in-depth study of young people working on computers and the Internet and how the media have changed their lives. This book will give you a good overview of children living and socializing in the "computer age."

Web sites of interest to students Several Web sites should interest your students:

- Whale songs at www.whales.ot.com
- Monterey Aquarium at www.mbayaq.org
- Exploratorium in San Francisco at www.exploratorium.edu

Other useful sites

The Eisenhower National Clearinghouse at www.enc.org is a site from Ohio State University linked to the Department of Education and is of particular interest to teachers. Here you'll find information on teacher recruitment and training, information on math and science and much more.

Not all Web sites you'll visit are free. Some sites charge after the first visit. Be aware of this.

Another good resource for K-12 teachers and students is the Electronic Library at www.education.elibrary.com. Here students can get into public libraries to view magazines and journals. This site has references and historical sources.

The "Weekly Reader" has a site at www.weeklyreader.com.

NOTE: Many school districts develop their own Web sites with links that have been reviewed by district personnel. Some districts have also developed use policy that outlines acceptable guidelines for using the Internet. For example, students' names are usually not used on-line.

Students and parents at many schools must sign a Student Internet Use Agreement.

Internet help for teachers Not only will your students receive help on the Internet but so will you. Teacher tools include ways to maintain grades, to write memos, do research and to develop curriculum. Here are a few outstanding Web sites.

- Instructor at www.scholastic.com. Choose from the home-page the topic you're looking for.
- Teachers' Education Online at www.teachnet.com
- To obtain links to many sites of interest to teachers, go to www.edweek.org for outstanding information.
- One such site is Eric Clearinghouse at www.cal.org/ericell with exceptional information for teachers on a variety of topics.
- Do a Web search with the keywords "lesson plans."

Ideas and resources for your classroom, including lesson plans for math, science, art and English, are a click away on the Internet. A good source I recommend is www.Eduzone.com.

When browsing on a Web page, look for other links to additional information.

HINT: Yahoo is an excellent search engine for Web sites and topics of interest. Use keywords such as "cornell university" and you'll receive their address at www.cornell.edu. On this page, you'll discover many teacher-friendly sites. Another helpful site is Houghton Mifflin at www.hmco.com/school/. Use other search engines such as WebCrawler and Alta Vista to locate more.

The following examples of technology can help with curriculum:

- Science—weather information, to compare and collect data
- Social Studies—history of local community and information on current issues
- Art—a variety of artistic tools
- Math—illustrates concepts on computers

Creative ideas for students to help design banners and posters can be found at the Magic 3-D Coloring site for children ages three to eight at www.us.pc.ibm.com/multimedia/.

A good place to see online newspapers written for students, by students, with excellent graphics and games, is www.little-planet.com.

For multicultural information with materials in twelve languages go to www.kidlink.org.

Many publishers provide laser disks and CD-ROMs to support their curriculum. Two are *National Geographic* and *The Audubon Society.*

These are only a few of the thousands of entertaining and educational Web sites available, and literally hundreds more are added each week.

A brief glossary of terms As you become more familiar with technology, you'll be amazed at all the new language you'll need to know. A few terms follow:

- WAIS: Wide Area Information Servers is a system of searchable text databases.
- WAN: Wide Area Network is a system of connected computers spanning a large area.
- LAN: Local Area Network is a network of computers confined within a small area like an office building.
- Multimedia is a combination of two or more media types including text, graphics, animation, audio and video to produce documents or other projects.
- A server is one-half of the client-server protocol, runs on a networked computer and responds to requests by the client.

Other issues The Internet has entered our homes and schools so quickly we need ways to address some of the accompanying issues:

- Copying material—Make your students aware of copyright restrictions.
- Ethics—Some districts have implemented agreement contracts between students and teachers regarding use of computers and the Web.
- Why use technology when the core curriculum at some schools is not even in place yet?
- The role of technology is constantly changing in our classrooms, in our labs and on the Net.

The downside of computers and the Internet in the classroom The computer and Internet are the "hot tools" for schools. Buying computers and going online is being pushed by parents and school districts.

Unfortunately, it's tremendously expensive to install computers, buy multimedia equipment and get students on the Internet. To find the money, some districts give up music programs, cut back on supplies and shortchange other programs.

At the same time, many districts don't budget sufficient money to service computers, provide teacher training and pay a mentor teacher to oversee the program.

Web sites come and go and new sites are added daily

The newest address throughout the world is "www" which means, "World Wide Web."

Your WWW browser is a client of the WWW server.

Some districts sponsor a "Net Day" when the community joins in to wire schools for computer use.

One state, to save money, asked state prisoners to wire its schools for computers. Some school districts float bonds and ask parents to help raise computer money. Even large corporations and local companies help underwrite this large expenditure in some areas.

While computers present wonderful learning opportunities, there are also ample opportunities for abuse—by shortchanging other school programs, by spending too much time on-line to do assigned work or enjoy other activities or by entering "adult-content" areas.

The upside of computers and the Internet in the classroom

While there is a downside from difficulties and growing pains regarding the use of computers and the Internet in the classroom, these problems must be addressed—*now*. They won't go away. Too many teachers and students have discovered the value of computers, and they insist they should be able to use these versatile tools—*now*. They're convinced the "technology of the future" has already arrived.

The voices of teachers, students and parents make it *urgent* for schools to develop technology plans for their classrooms. They must determine how staff development will be addressed, how equipment will be acquired and how all this new and existing technology can be combined and implemented in the most efficient manner.

NOTE: Many textbook publishers now provide software that ties directly to the curriculum and requires computer use. How will you use it?

Not only are publishers changing the textbook scene with computer software, but teachers are also taking advantage of their versatility. They're using computers to:

- Send home weekly memos to parents
- Record information on laptop computers at plan-writing meetings

If telephone and power lines aren't already in classrooms or aren't in sufficient quantity, they must be installed for computers and modems.

Only 20 percent of teachers have even basic computer training.

The school needs a technology committee to oversee the plan.

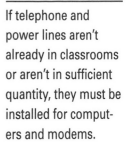

- Keep up-to-date records on students' grades, attendance and anecdotal notes, as needed
- Log onto the Internet for help with lesson planning, chat with other teachers or look for a job

Since that cold January morning in the '80s when I first rolled a single computer on a cart into my classroom, the changes in technology have been unbelievable.

Computers have changed and new methods and strategies have also developed for their utilization in the past few years. When I first experimented with a computer in the classroom, it was a novelty and most exciting. I, along with many teachers, were pioneers in searching for ways to convert this "new invention" to an educational tool for students.

Today not only must we learn to utilize this vast selection of equipment available for classrooms, but we must, at the same time, protect these valuable acquisitions.

 CAUTION: Before bringing a laptop, CD player, or stereo from home and into the classroom, be sure to use an electric pen to inscribe your driver's license number on each piece of equipment.

Also, in many places you'll need to take these valuables home with you at night. Consider locking your personal equipment in the trunk of your car each night upon leaving the classroom, providing you have a safe place to park your car. Teachers do this more and more in high-crime areas.

I failed to take mine home and lost valuable personal equipment one night when a fire was set in the school's faculty room where my small office was located. Be aware that the unexpected can, and sometimes does, happen.

In the workplace we're seeing a lack of young women going into computer fields.

Technology can be a boon for your classroom. But it's essential you receive training and keep up-to-date with the changing technological landscape. Also, encourage all your students, but particularly the girls, to become computer literate and to use this tool properly. Students' working futures may well be dependent upon this skill.

Issues in Education

I*ntroduction* This is a time of transition in education. Many of the topics I'll address in this chapter have no firm answers and in the years to come, we'll continue to struggle to find answers.

Our classrooms change from day to day. We're a nation of many languages and ethnic groups, with large school districts having as many as 100 different groups to teach.

At the same time, we're seeing a growing gap between the rich and the poor in this country. This is reflected in our schools, in our national dialog and is observed daily by teachers in the classroom.

This chapter's brief overview of many of our pressing educational issues will help you better understand what is going on in your classroom, your community and throughout the country.

Parent Involvement

By age five, children have learned half of what they will ever learn. Yes, parents are important.

For years, as a teacher, I'd struggle with children reading and speaking poorly and parents not caring. On February 19, 1996, *Newsweek* featured an article called "Your Child's Brain." After reading the article, I realized the importance of adults interacting with *all* youngsters at an early age.

Contents

HINT: Make several copies of this article at your library for yourself and interested parents. Along with good information, it provides a timeline indicating when to introduce language, math, emotional control, social interaction and a second language to youngsters.

Parents need to know that their baby needs ongoing holding, talking, laughing and singing to activate its millions of brain neurons.

The neurons are like keys on a computer keyboard. "The keys that are typed—the experiences a child has—determine whether the child grows up to be intelligent or dull, fearful or self-assured, articulate or tongue-tied," says Harry Chugani of Wayne State University. "They can completely change the way a person turns out."

 NOTE: I had a seven-year-old student who couldn't speak, read or write. During his early years his mother, a prostitute and drug addict, had mostly left him alone with little interaction.

It took the resources of seven staff people to help the youngster, and his prognosis is still not good. You also may come in contact with these "throw-away" children. Get help as quickly as possible.

More and more school districts are picking up the slack of uncaring parents by opening free preschools for all children, regardless of economic status.

Teachers and parents need to be aware of the importance of working with babies at an early age and continuing this interest as youngsters progress through the grades. Unfortunately, at the same time we are learning the critical importance of parent-child interaction, more and more parents seem to be less and less available.

"The number-one change for school children in recent years," says one veteran principal, "is that stay-at-home mothers have moved into full time jobs. Today we see the PTA disintegrating, homework not being checked and fewer volunteers in classrooms."

Yet in some parts of the country this trend is being reversed. In greater Los Angeles, thirteen schools have been designated "family schools" which parents and children attend together on Saturdays.

Computers were bought, parent centers opened and teacher-training programs begun with help from local universities. "We are trying to create a community of learners that extends beyond the traditional school doors," says Constance Gibson, a principal in Van Nuys, California.

On Saturdays, 300 children study math, science, art or karate, while 90 parents learn to use computers, take English classes and sign up to do volunteer work at the school.

In other places, school districts are installing voice-mail systems so busy working parents can keep in touch with their child's teacher and leave messages any time, day or night. Some parents want to know about their children's behavior problems and missed homework assignments.

Even though parents are busy, they need to attend parent meetings and conferences. Otherwise, children begin to see school as not important. You may find this means evening meetings with parents.

"If the parent has a positive attitude toward school," says one administrator, "Then the child will see it is important—not always fun, perhaps, but a good place to learn and grow."

Use Parent Conferences and Back-To-School Nights to encourage parents to model good school habits such as taking classes and reading at home. Remind parents they are their child's first teacher and every child needs both a coach and cheerleader.

"All a child needs," says Diane Ackerman—poet, essayist, and naturalist, "is one adult who believes in the child, who conveys a sense of encouragement and faith, for the child to prevail."

Model for a Good School

A good school is a community of parents, teachers, students, aides, volunteers and a principal with a positive, shared vision.

The ideal principal is passionate about the job, has compassion for others, uses a positive problem-solving approach to difficulties and supports the staff in obtaining resources for special projects.

At a good school the teachers, no matter what their age or experience, enjoy the challenge of working with children. They not only prepare students for standardized tests but for the real world as well.

Good schools also work hard to be sure all students have access to computers. These might be in labs or in the classrooms.

"The number-one indicator of a child's success in school is parent involvement."

Christine Olsen, San Juan Unified School District, CA

If teaching in a crime area, check with your school office to be sure it's safe to be on the campus at night. Also, take a friend along and alert the custodian that you'll be at school.

The parents' attitude toward school is important, as it reflects how their child will feel about it.

Parents need to teach children to act civilized.

More and more "good schools" are seeing the need for a school-uniform policy.

All youngsters, no matter their economic status, should grow up with their hands on a mouse.

Good schools recruit teachers to match their students' cultures.

- More minority teachers are needed.
- Schools need more men, especially in kindergarten and the primary grades, to serve as role models.

Good schools actively seek parents and grandparents to volunteer there. Principals also go into middle and nearby high schools and ask students to volunteer to help young students read.

High schoolers at one good school work with nearby kindergartners on phonemic awareness, which is the ability to recognize all sounds that a word contains. As many as 15 to 20 percent of these kindergartners were never read to as toddlers, and high schoolers help fill the need.

Good schools also encourage fathers to participate in their children's education. Recent surveys indicate that students are more apt to get "A's" and less likely to repeat a grade or be expelled if their fathers are actively involved in their education. This means the fathers attend school meetings and parent conferences, and even volunteer at school.

Charter Schools

Charter Schools have been around for a hundred years and are generally authorized by individual state legislatures. A particular school then petitions the local district to become a Charter School. The *Charter School Act* of 1992 in California, for example, encourages school boards and schools to "think outside the 'box' to find solutions to help all students learn."

A typical charter states the school will:

- Operate independently as a school within the school district
- Have staff continue to be district employees
- Continue to educate district students

Charter Schools provide a setting in which to operate without the heavy bureaucracy often found in large districts.

At one Charter School, accomplishments in literacy were made by adding reading coaches to the staff and putting in place a reading-incentive program to motivate students to read. The library was also upgraded and students participated in the Young Author Program.

A Charter School board is directed by a steering committee made up of parents, certificated and classified representatives and the principal. The charter allows:

- Better control over funding and expense resources
- Control over the daily and yearly schedules

How do teacher benefits compare at Charter and other district schools? Generally the pay, monetary benefits and seniority rights are the same. However, at Charter Schools, a "family" atmosphere develops, leading to group decisions about goals, discipline and learning climate, school safety, school environment, parent involvement and more.

Some Charter Schools are very large within metropolitan school districts. Others are small, yet all have the goal to help children achieve their best.

Magnet Schools

A Magnet School is one which includes specialized curricula ranging from math to science to a foreign language. The Magnet School is not run by a charter but through the school district.

The problem with a number of Magnet Schools is that they are too popular and have long waiting lists.

Problems develop when:
- There are too few slots for neighborhood children and for disadvantaged and minority students.
- Some schools require that parents provide transportation.
- The school can rise and fall with the commitment of the principal and parents.

Enrolling a child in a Magnet School is particularly difficult for non-English-speaking parents. The paperwork can be overwhelming, due dates must be honored and parents often lack transportation for their children.

Those praising Magnet Schools point out that the school is for everyone and that highly motivated students often out-perform conventional public-school children on tests.

Private Schools

Private schools can be religious, privately run-for-profit or cultural.

Advocates for public-versus-private schools are often unhappy when Congress deals with private-school issues. While only 14 percent of American families place their children in private schools, surveys indicated that 34 percent of House members

---

At Charter Schools, teachers feel they have more control over their teaching day.

The principal at one Charter School explains that the staff insists every child can learn and every teacher can become an excellent teacher.

Many students do better when they focus on a theme they enjoy.

Some parents see Magnet Schools as their only means for getting their child into a private-type school at government expense.

In one large district, only six percent of all students attend a Magnet School.

In one large school district, 70,000 students applied for 13,000 Magnet-School slots.

and 50 percent of the Senate had their own children in private schools.

Why do people send their children to private schools?

- Classes are usually smaller.
- Parents feel their children will be safer.
- Values will be taught in religious schools.
- There's more exchange between teachers and students.
- School hours better fit working parents' schedules.
- The longer kindergarten day in private schools helps working parents cut down on additional child care.

New teachers teaching in private schools In the past few years, salaries have gone up for teachers in private schools. However, before signing a contract, future teachers need to be informed regarding:

- Health benefits
- Retirement plans
- Salary comparison with that of public schools
- Amount of parent participation

Many teachers enjoy teaching in a private school, as it becomes a close family unit. They not only see each other at school but often socialize together. The teachers care about each other and work together to help each child develop both academically and emotionally.

School Vouchers

By definition, school vouchers are cash stipends that can be used to pay for a child's private-school tuition.

Milwaukee, Wisconsin, and Cleveland, Ohio, have used tax dollars for several years to supply vouchers for students wishing to attend private schools. It's reported only about 20,000 students throughout the country, are attending schools on vouchers.

Some investors in the private sector are pledging funds for needy students to go to private schools.

With 52 million children in public schools and only eight million in private schools, many parents are urging members of Congress to supply vouchers for their children. This is particularly true in black inner-city communities where parents wish to provide a better education for their children.

However, in white suburbia where schools are often well-funded and have much parent involvement, the idea is not at all popular. The plan to use their tax dollars to send other children to private schools is loudly questioned.

Critics of the voucher system are also concerned that moving large numbers of students into private schools will leave public schools without necessary funds to educate their children.

The voucher battle continues to rage in Congress between Democrats and Republicans and between public and religious schools. Many church and parochial schools indicate their interest in being part of the voucher system, but this leads to heated discussions about using federal-tax dollars for these church-related schools. Despite the battles, polls indicate more public acceptance toward voucher use. Recent surveys also show *more* public concern about putting a computer into every classroom and using national standards to measure the academic performance of children.

Home Schools

Homeschooling is growing throughout the country, both in rural and urban areas. Estimates are that one million or more children are homeschooled each day.

When the family is far from public schools, there's often little choice. But other parents make this considerable commitment for varying reasons, including:

- They can teach their own values.
- Some schools are not safe.
- They are concerned about drugs and gangs.
- Their child can spend more time on his or her special interests such as music or science.
- Home can be less materialistic with no brand-name clothes or other expensive possessions.

Learning at home often works well as the parent can teach to the child's learning style. That might be auditory, visual or kinesthetic. The one-on-one approach is helpful for teaching all subjects.

To legally homeschool, the parent needs to work under some official school umbrella. In many cases, parents file papers with their local county or school district to operate as a private school. In others, the child is enrolled in an independent-study program. Church schools also may support home teaching.

The parent's learning style is often the same as the child's.

Many parents who homeschool find it valuable to network with others. This could include joining other homeschoolers for physical-education activities, field trips or enrolling children in a nearby music program. Sometimes parents with specialized training present regular group lessons on science, for example, or algebra or calculus.

Homeschool materials are plentiful. They can be obtained from several sources:

- Garage sales
- Public libraries
- Mail order
- Homeschool conventions
- School districts' homeschool programs
- The Internet

Student schedules may vary but districts generally provide guidelines for the number of hours to be spent on specific subjects. Many districts also test children during the school year when parents teach under the school-district umbrella.

Family vacations can serve as extended field trips. In a number of homes, the student is part of a family enterprise and homeschooling is scheduled around working on family projects. Students find that volunteer time at libraries or hospitals also provides opportunities to interact with others and develop responsibility.

These days many homeschoolers spend more time on computers and the Internet. They do reports, gain information off the Net and plug into libraries across the country for additional resources.

Some homeschoolers return to the classroom It's not unusual for some homeschoolers to return to the classroom. One reason often given is the parent chooses to no longer homeschool the child. This may be due to the student reaching an advanced grade. But the transition from home to conventional school can sometimes be traumatic for both student and teacher.

NOTE: When a homeschooled child enrolls in your classroom, recognize he or she has had freedom to move from place-to-place and may not have worked on a set schedule. Also, there probably has been no need to cooperate with other students.

Conduct a parent-teacher-child conference prior to the youngster entering the classroom and prepare for the transition. Discuss your rules and procedures and provide a handout of your class schedule and rules for the parent and child to discuss at home.

"Within one week I had two home-schooled youngsters come into my third-grade room. Both were barely reading at first-grade level."

An elementary teacher

"I've had former homeschoolers leave my room without my knowledge and wander the schoolgrounds. This, for legal and safety reasons, must not happen."

An elementary teacher

Assign a student to "shepherd" the new youngster through the first two weeks of school. This means walking with the new student to the restroom, cafeteria and library and answering questions regarding school procedures.

While homeschooling can be a positive experience, teachers and parents must anticipate the problems which sometimes arise when the child enters a classroom afterward.

Values

In the '80s, schools weren't allowed to discuss character and morals with students. By the '90s, behavior problems began to interfere with a teacher's ability to teach and the children's opportunity to learn. As a result, many parents now demand that schools teach values. In surveys, parents say to teach:

- Honesty
- Respect
- Morality
- Responsibility

Several large school districts which have started teaching values report a drop in behavior problems at their schools. As a new teacher, you may be asked to teach values and it will seem to be one more duty in an already busy schedule. For this reason, many districts work with teachers to integrate values into the daily school program. This might be done during Social Studies or through literature.

Values can also be expressed in journal writing and used as part of the vocabulary words in language classes.

➤ NOTE: Students must be taught to be respectful of those who don't share their same values. With several religions and cultures represented in the same classroom, other points of view must be respected.

A particularly useful resource to have in your room is *Teaching Your Children Values* by Linda and Richard Eyre. The book details simple lesson plans for presenting a variety of character issues.

Attention Deficit Disorder (ADD)

It's estimated that between five and seven percent of all students have a problem processing information.

In a recent survey, 80 percent of students said they lied and cheated at school to get ahead.

A good place to teach and model honesty, respect and responsibility is during Class Meetings.

ADD students are often bright and witty.

Kindergarten teachers are good at identifying students outside the norm.

ADHD means attention deficit with hyperactivity.

Students moving from place-to-place in classrooms which use learning centers can be distracting.

ADD students pay attention and enjoy things they find stimulating, such as video games, but they often function poorly in the classroom.

ADD boys act out; girls check out—they daydream.

Out of the total number of ADD students, about 60 percent are boys and 40 percent are girls.

A specialist in ADD explains that behavior modification does not work with these students, but firm and consistent discipline does.

The problem, according to a specialist in the field of ADD, lies within the brain. Information is processed slowly, while at the same time, these students become easily distracted.

These youngsters appear to be able to work on only one mental process at a time and are easily distracted by sounds and movement. For example, the loud ticking of a clock, a bird flying around outside the classroom, or even a pencil dropping, can upset the processing of information.

ADD students may excel at absorbing single-function activities such as playing Nintendo™ but do poorly in the classroom with many students and distractions.

ADD students often do better in a classroom when working in cubbyholes separated by partitions, but cubbyholes are seldom used now. The ideal solution is to insulate your ADD students from distractions without seeming to isolate or punish them.

The next best place is at a desk near you. When you give directions, give them to the entire class, and then stand near your ADD student and give the directions again.

Overall, ADD students have to try harder to do things than other students and by the second and third grades, with added academic pressure, they begin to act out. Therefore, it's important to draw attention to the *good* things they do.

If you suspect a student may have ADD, contact the school nurse and counselor for help. They, in turn, may ask the family to see a doctor.

"First of all," says a pediatrician, "I educate the parents on how to handle and work with their child at home." If that doesn't work, the doctor might move on to medication.

Bilingual Education

This topic is guaranteed to raise heat wherever it's discussed. Whether it's teachers, parents, school boards or the public at large, all are vocal on this subject.

Bilingual education began about twenty years ago as a way to help non-English-speaking children make a smooth transition into the classroom. But many critics now claim that teaching students in their native tongue hampers their mastery of English. Some want total English immersion from the first day of school to end bilingual education completely. Others favor a special program for one, three, five or seven years.

How schools meet the needs of bilingual students States and school districts meet the needs of limited-English students in several ways. In some primary classrooms, the teacher speaks both Spanish and English. She gives directions in both languages and later meets with her Spanish speakers to answer any questions they might have.

At other schools, students are taught English in the morning and Spanish in the afternoon. At one school, a retired man who speaks Spanish, heads a "pullout" program. Children who need help with English work in small groups on math, reading and writing.

Teaching bilingual students Depending upon your state and school district, two ways to receive a certificate to teach bilingual students are:

- Take prescribed classes and pass a test on bilingual skills.
- Have sufficient knowledge of the language and culture to pass a test.

Parental concern about bilingual programs More and more parents are refusing to have their children in bilingual classes. Other parents have joined together in marches to illustrate their unhappiness with the programs. These parents want their children to learn English now so they can better fit into mainstream society and not be dependent later upon migratory farm or other minimum-wage work.

At the same time, school districts are faced with high dropout rates for Hispanic students. At 30 percent nationwide, this is a higher rate than for either black or white students leaving school. Many troubled students say they leave because:

- They're failing.
- They're bored.
- They're working to support their families.

While there are no easy answers for how or how long to teach bilingual students, or how to stop the high dropout rate among some minorities, many schools still try hard to meet the needs of all students. Sometimes they labor in impossible situations. In one Virginia school district alone, students come from 182 countries and speak 100 different languages.

As the numbers of bilingual students grow, schools across the country will continue to seek ways to include them in the American mainstream of society. Mastering English appears to be the best way to achieve this goal.

Whatever their native tongue, every child needs a common social language. For example, "Where's the bathroom?" Or, "What does the cafeteria have for lunch today?"

Bilingual students, based on their English language skills, are designated:
• Beginners
• Intermediates
• Advanced

The faces of education change with every famine and every war.

Effective bilingual education must start early and be intensive in teaching English.

Special Education

A "Special-Ed" classroom is one where children who need special help receive assistance. These students may be considered:

- Learning Handicapped—Students who have problems with language, memory, concentration, following directions and reading.

- Severely Handicapped—Students who have serious retardation and have delayed adaptive behavior. This might be a six-year-old who can't put on his or her shoes.

- Communicatively Handicapped—Children with serious delays in language. They're unable to express thoughts, or the language is scrambled in their brains.

- Orthopedically Handicapped—Students with physical limitations which might require a wheelchair, crutches or a walker. These students are often served in a regular classroom.

- Emotionally Disturbed—Children with serious behavior problems which prevent them from learning and getting along with others for a long period of time. This category can be difficult to assess.

☛ NOTE: Some of these children might be together in one room but not from all categories at once.

The term "mainstream" means to place students with special problems in general-education classes yet still provide them with appropriate instruction support. In most cases, mainstreaming takes place for a portion of the day with the student spending the remainder of the day in a special-education classroom.

These days there's a movement toward "full inclusion" which merges special education and regular education. The children with problems are fully integrated into the education program. Here, the extra support needed *comes* to the student rather than *pulling* the youngster out of the classroom for additional help.

Credential requirements In order to work with Learning-Handicapped students, teachers in many states must obtain a credential which usually requires 42 more units of course work. To work with Severely Handicapped students, a credential which requires 41 units is needed. The courses cover legal aspects, consultation, assessment, instruction design, behavior management, cultural linguistic diversity and student teaching.

Special-education students generally have an Individual Education Plan in place with the specific goals and objectives they are working on. However, many teachers work with other class-

Some special education teachers must write 15 different lesson plans just for math.

It's difficult for many intermediate students in special education to go into regular classrooms as they often have problems with reading and writing.

rooms on joint projects such as a "Buddy Up" program. Here youngsters might join regular classes for physical education, art and math.

Special-education classes work under the umbrella of the Disabilities Education Act which is a federal law detailing specific requirements to be met.

In recent years, students participating in federal programs have increased by 46 percent while funding has gone down. The number of students in the program with specific learning problems has doubled, while those with speech and language impairments or mental retardation have decreased.

In states where the special-education population is substantial, school budgets have been severely strained. Many complaints about decreased funding allotments are being heard throughout the country.

Mandated Testing for Students

Mandated testing for all students is another "hot button." One suggestion being considered is voluntary testing for all fourth and eighth graders in math. Numerous concerns start with, "Which test to use?"

- A government-developed test?
- Existing state tests?
- Commercial tests?

At the same time, both teachers and parents are concerned that students are already being "tested to death."

In Chicago the district requires all students in grades three, six, eight and nine to pass standardized tests in order to promote to the next grade. Not all principals in Chicago agree, though, and one suggests, "These students could drown in tests." Teachers explain:

- Class time must be spent getting ready for tests.
- The media can misconstrue test results.
- Constant testing results in anxiety among students.

"Who will do the testing?" is another problem area. State and local school districts declare they should do it, while at the same time, questions are asked about the test materials. Who determines what is worth knowing and what should be on a test?

Special-education students represent more than ten percent of total school enrollment.

"What do you mean by higher national standards? What about Head Start so that all children start school with a full stomach? What about giving them homes that are drug-free? Are those part of your national standards?"

A teacher in Seattle

"First graders taking tests were crying, getting stomachaches and having nightmares."

Professor of Education

On average, students take from three to nine tests each year.

As with many other issues in education, student testing is political and creates debates and tensions within Congress, in school districts and among parents. With over $15 million in federal funds needed to even begin the testing process, more and more groups are expressing concerns which, no doubt, will continue.

Social Promotion of Students

Many school districts require mandated testing at specific grade levels, but not all. Others ask that students pass a test in order to move on to the next grade level. Again, not all districts do this. All too often students move to the next grade without the necessary skills in place and this is called, "social promotion."

Social promotion simply means passing a student on to the next grade just for spending time in classes. Chicago schools are taking a long look at this "dirty little secret in education" and are now placing requirements upon low-achieving students if they don't pass the test for promotion.

First-aid possibilities for students who don't meet requirements:

- Go to summer school.
- Repeat a grade.
- Enroll in an intervention program after early identification.
- Participate in an intensive catch-up program.
- Enroll in a summer tutorial program.

One problem often faced by school districts regarding social promotion is that later on, students who fail have a much higher dropout rate than others.

Many critics loudly argue against mandated testing programs. They claim urban and minority students are unfairly targeted because they're often bad test takers. Some congressmen cite these testing methods as being "Draconian."

However, in districts where summer school, tutorials and intervention are used, results show test scores going up and students scholastically able to move on to the next grade.

Mandated Teacher Testing

At a time when thousands of teachers are being hired nationwide, many lack qualifications for the job. A survey conducted by the National Commission on Teaching and America's Future, indicates over one-fourth had not completed their license requirements in their main teaching areas.

"Testing blows almost a full month of school."

Supervisor of student teachers

Some parents are suing school districts for retaining their children for low test scores.

"There are no social promotions in life."

Thomas Reese, Teachers' Union

Mandated teacher testing continues to be discussed in faculty rooms, Congress and the executive branch of government. Several states are considering mandated testing of all teachers, yet no national consensus has been reached as to what the tests will include. At the same time, the Carnegie Corporation established a national board to set certification standards in 1987. Teachers are asked by the National Board for Professional Teaching Standards to volunteer for the testing.

Questions arise at school districts over the cost of $2,000 apiece for teachers, like lawyers and doctors, to become board-certified. Some teachers pay the cost themselves, while others look to their school districts for assistance.

This process also raises the question of merit pay for certain teachers. Some districts won't reward board-certified teachers, while others give a 15 percent pay increase for certification.

As interest increases in becoming board-certified, some colleges and universities are offering classes to prepare teachers for the recommended testing.

The Secretary of Education admits that schools have lowered their standards to fill teaching slots but has warned that this practice must end.

In order for all students to learn, every teacher must be prepared and qualified to teach. Teachers' unions, Congress and teachers all need to work together to provide the best possible education for this nation's children.

Personal Issues in Teaching

The personal puzzle pieces Modern education is like a complex puzzle. It resembles the pieces on the apple you see on the cover of this book. At times, the focus is on handwriting and spelling, later on computers and frequently on how to show student progress on a report card.

During your years of teaching, many changes will take place. At times you'll feel discouraged with the transitions you're asked to go through, but don't give up. You can help and influence so many more children than you realize in your day-to-day work.

Keep in mind that many voices will form the patterns of change and in many cases, you'll have little input, but you're still a teacher. Some of the changes will come from:

- Your state legislature
- Your school board

- The school superintendent
- The school principal
- The school steering committee
- You as the teacher

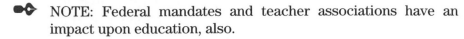 NOTE: Federal mandates and teacher associations have an impact upon education, also.

As changes take place, you must remain flexible and be willing not only for these to occur, but you must also prepare for them. This might be taking additional classes in a new reading or math program. It might be a workshop on the latest methods for working with computers in the classroom.

You'll also have some personal decisions to make. Do you wish to spend your entire career teaching at one school and one grade level? Since my personality is such that I needed variety in my life, I changed schools and grade levels about every five years.

By doing this I met new people, worked with children of different ages and taught new and different materials. I always enjoyed the challenge. You may not, but this is for you to decide.

In the end, no matter what educational wind is blowing, you are your students' teacher. It's still your responsibility to shape and motivate the young lives you teach every day. Be the best you can and enjoy the journey.

References and Additional Reading

Ellis, Susan, and Whalen, Susan (1990). *Cooperative Learning, Getting Started.* New York: Scholastic.

Favors, John; and Favors, Kathryne (1994). *Thematic Integrated Education.* Sacramento, CA: Jonka Enterprises.

Hayes, Deborah (1995). *Managing Technology in the Classroom.* Huntington Beach, CA: Teacher Created Materials, Inc.

Hayes, Deborah (1997). *Multimedia Projects.* Huntington Beach, CA: Teacher Created Materials, Inc.

Jones, Fredric (1987). *Positive Classroom Discipline.* New York: McGraw-Hill Book Company.

Kagan, Spencer (1994). *Cooperative Learning.* San Clemente, CA: Kagan Cooperative Learning.

Kagan, Spencer, Laurie and Miguel (1997). *Teambuilding.* San Clemente, CA: Kagan Cooperative Learning.

Kellough, Richard (1997). *A Resource Guide for Teaching: K-12, Second Edition.* Upper Saddle River, NJ: Prentice Hall, Inc.

Kohn, Alfie (1993). *Punished by Rewards.* Boston, MA: Houghton Mifflin Company.

Kronowitz, Ellen (1996). *Your First Year of Teaching and Beyond, Second Edition.* White Plains, NY: Longman Publishers USA.

Levine, John; Baroudi, Carol, Young, Margaret, and Bender, Hy, (1997). *The Internet for Dummies®. Foster City, CA:* IDA Books Worldwide.

Rosengart, Terry (1997). *ClarisWorks® for Terrified Teachers.* Huntington Beach, CA: Teacher Created Materials, Inc.

Rosengart, Terry (1996). *Writing and Desktop Publishing on the Computer.* Huntington Beach, CA: Teacher Created Materials, Inc.

Tapscott, Don (1998). *Growing Up Digital.* New York: McGraw-Hill.

Thompson, Gare (1991). *Teaching Through Themes,* New York, Scholastic.

Index